DEDICATION

Sarah dedicates this book to a lively patriot who lives a life worthy of storytelling, Virginia Hare. A few of her adventures are recorded here.

Virginia dedicates this book to Rabbit who prepared her to live alone and be independent, even as a new bride.

And

To the gals of Dami Phi Datum whose enduring friendships added zest to her life and who hammered her for years to write a book.
Roger that, Virginia!

COVER PHOTO: The first Dami Phi reunion at Phoenix's Encanto Park, December 1959. Virginia, Mary Lou, Snookie, Shirley, and Barbara along with all of their children enjoyed a special, memorable day together.

Table of Contents

Virginia's Family Twenty Years Earlier 7
Growth and Opportunity 25
The Girls of Dami Phi Datum 33
The Dami Phi Datum Charter 41
Dami Phi News, Volume I, August 31, 1949 51
From Dami Phi Datum to Don't Mindi Phi Du 61
"Rabbit" Hare 93
Plans and Reality Collide......................................103
Marriage! What Have I Gotten Into?...................111
The Dope 121
Germany 129
France 141
Home Again, Sort Of 153
A Graduation Picture for the Broken Frame 181
Dami Phi Reunions 195
Dami Phi Legacy...215
Afterword – Where Are They Now?....................227
Acknowledgements..237

Published by McKinley Browne Publishing in Oklahoma City, Oklahoma
McKinleyBrowne.com

ISBN-13: 978-0-9885850-8-9
ISBN-10: 0988585081

Design & Layout: Scott Horton

The Girls of
DAMI PHI DATUM

67 years of life and friendship

by

SARAH HORTON

with VIRGINIA HARE

MCKINLEY BROWNE PUBLISHING

The Girls of

DAMI PHI DATUM

---

67 years of life and friendship

by

SARAH HORTON

with VIRGINIA HARE

MCKINLEY BROWNE PUBLISHING

Prologue – The Beginning

The wheels of the 1939 single bench-seat Chevy coupe screeched to a halt by the Phoenix Labor Temple. The wide, curvaceous front fenders and oversized chrome grill made the car horribly dated since the new 1950 design hit the streets of Phoenix, Arizona; but the overload of passengers didn't care. Six, maybe seven, beautiful high school girls spilled from the doors like clowns in a circus. Chatter and giggles filled the night air as they made their way to the Johnson's apartment behind the labor union offices.

Shirley Johnson's mother was out of town, consequently, the girls spoke freely about the frustrating nature of boys. The girls brimmed with excitement to be a part of forming this new group. Shirley and her boyfriend, Bob Cannon had broken up, again; Shirley had had enough. Things were going to change; she was going to change. This night was the beginning, not only for Shirley, but for the others too. Virginia Howell, Snookie Lintz, Martha Martin, Mary Lou

Henson, and Barbara Witten looked to their futures with great expectation.

Shirley called the girls to order. She laid out the purpose of the group to support each other in shifting their focus from boys to academics and planning for a bright future. They agreed to a one date each month rule and a "good girl" pledge. Shirley announced the name of the club that immediately put the good girl pledge to the test . . .

DAMI PHI DATUM!

The giggling young girls never considered that they would continue to be known by that name more than sixty years later.

Virginia's Family Twenty Years Earlier

Thrilled to be in the thriving city of Phoenix, Ruth McLeland Howell prepared to embrace her new life as Harold's bride. The country girl from Nebraska dreamed big dreams. Not many girls thought of becoming a doctor in the 1920s and even fewer farm girls considered such a professional post a possibility. Maybe her aspirations were the very thing that set young Ruth apart when the man from Phoenix came to visit. Well, that and her beauty, hardly disguised by the stained apron tied around her waist.

Ruth's mother was pregnant with her tenth child and could no longer meet the demands of cooking for her large family and the thirty some-odd farm hands expecting sustenance for their labor. It was decided the family and the farm needed Ruth more than Ruth needed a high school diploma. At the age of seventeen Ruth saw that apron as a straight jacket, which became her wardrobe staple. It was her captivity. Two years in the hot kitchen with only farm hands and younger siblings for company made newcomer Harold more interesting.

Eleven years her senior, Harold knew all too well the desire to escape a life of bondage. Generations of Howells before him performed the hard and dangerous work of coal mining in Ohio. Those who survived the mines eventually succumbed to the copious cough and sparse breath of lungs blackened by coal dust. At the age of twenty, Harold traded the black coal of Ohio for the black asphalt of Arizona. Constructing highways in the desert was not necessarily easier than the work of a coal miner, but the hot, dry air was clean, abundant, and free.

Harold met the pretty girl on a visit to Nebraska, and could think of only one way to get her to Phoenix. Ruth quickly untied her knotted apron to tie a knot of a different sort with Harold. The newlyweds purchased a two-bedroom frame house sitting on one and a half acres of Arizona desert. It lay near the capitol city and was filled with opportunity and promise.

They adopted Let The Rest of The World Go

By as their theme song from that moment forward. Ruth would begin and Harold would join in with her singing:

"With someone like you, a pal good and true, I'd like to leave it all behind and go and find a place that's known to God alone. Just a spot we could call our own. We'll find perfect peace, where joys never cease, somewhere beneath the starry skies. We'll build a sweet little nest somewhere in the west, and let the rest of the world go by."

The young couple had no holdings in the stock market that crashed only one year before they wed. Although they suffered no personal loss of investments, no one was insulated from the scarcity of money and the escalating rate of unemployment. Harold knew he was fortunate to have a job. His career traveled from working the highways of Arizona to the Plymouth Dodge automotive dealership in downtown Phoenix. He repainted cars for owners Ed and Bert Spears in exchange for ten dollars each week. He perfected his craft while Ruth set about turning their parcel of earth into something so fruitful and lush to rival a productive Nebraska farm.

Harold and Ruth owned their property and home located in the rural area called the Four Boy Eighty, named after the four Sloan boys and the eighty acres Mr. Sloan had subdivided. Harold's salary was just enough to cover taxes, food, and transportation. Any extra money was invested in trees for the orchard that added some security and peace of mind; if Harold lost his job as one out of every four men did, during this time they would have something to eat. This type of security grew in importance as they made plans to expand their family.

After three years of marriage, a tiny bundle was placed into Ruth's loving arms. They decided to call her Virginia Ruth and willingly gave their hearts to the closest thing to perfect either of them had ever experienced. The abundant joy little Virginia brought into Ruth's life was off set by the mountain of cotton diapers in constant need of washing. The strain of the workload did not go unnoticed by Harold who splurged an entire week's pay on a Maytag wringer washer.

The motorized machine saved Ruth back-breaking labor. All she had to do each washday was build a fire in the outdoor pit to heat water in what was once her washtub. She added the hot water to the round grey tub with a red Maytag logo printed on the front. Diapers were first rinsed then added one piece at a time to prevent over-filling the machine. When she was satisfied with the size of the load, Ruth added soap and let the motor do the work. A few minutes later she returned to stop the agitator, turn on the wringer, and feed each article of clothing through the turning cylinders to squeeze out the excess water and soap. A rinse in clean water followed with another round of feeding each article through the wringer. Clothespins then secured laundry to the tightly stretched line until it was dry. Ruth carefully pressed each piece free of wrinkles and set it ready to be worn. Needless to say, Ruth was eager to potty train Virginia soon after she began to walk!

The family's small home that once provided warmth and coziness suddenly felt smaller with Virginia on the move. Side-stepping around soft, pudgy feet while rearranging objects to protect her unsteady gait soon gave evidence to the need for more space. Plans for a new home took shape.

Harold and Ruth shared an appreciation for quality that reflected in the construction of their new house, beginning with a slab foundation. The slab was more solid and dependable than the commonly used block supports with a crawl space, which prevented insulation from the sun's scorching ground temperatures. Mexican laborers skillfully molded adobe bricks to serve as the walls of their new home. Virginia watched the men dig the rich soil, add just the right amount of straw, moisten it to a pliable mud, then pat it and shape it in preparation for the sun's natural oven to do the baking. As the bricks piled up, the hole grew until it swallowed the men alive only to spit them back out again with mud in hand to form even more bricks.

Harold's efforts to dig two cesspools provided even more dirt for the brick making. Once the hole reached a depth of more than seven feet, the family worked together at night by lamplight to line the cesspool cavern with bricks. Harold stationed himself in the hole while Ruth and Virginia carried bricks from the brick maker's pile to him. Ruth easily carried two bricks at a time while Virginia struggled with one. Proud to help with such important work, Virginia beamed until her small fingers lost their grip on a heavy brick. Gravity quickly guided the hardened, dried mud onto Harold's head. Virginia heard her daddy say words she was not allowed to repeat.

When the family wasn't working together building their new home, sometimes Virginia walked to visit the neighbors. The Parrack house sat high on blocks. Virginia's little legs strained to reach the top of the steps while her hands carefully maintained their grip on her Peter Rabbit book. At the Parrack's, she received buckets full of attention from four teenagers, the twins Anna 'n Mary, Matt, Leah, and their mother, too. They always had time to listen to her read and patiently answered her free flow of questions. They enjoyed being the audience for the only pre-schooler in the neighborhood. From their front porch perch, Virginia could glance over to continue supervising the construction work taking place on her property.

After her third birthday, Virginia's family moved into what was now the nicest house on 31st Avenue, a name that seems a little fancy for the rural, dirt road that it was. Thick adobe walls cooled the brutal summer heat and insulated warmth on cold winter nights. Area rugs softened scored concrete floors that were tinted red on one side of the house and green on the other. This became the grounds for acrobatics. Ruth lay on her back while Virginia flew through the air and flipped off the top of her mom's flexed feet. Harold joined in the fun, and laughter bounced off the walls.

Inside the home was a haven of happiness, while outside, the one and a half acres was a true desert oasis. Nearly anything could grow in the fertile soil and bountiful sunshine, but only if there was water. Phoenix built an infrastructure of irrigation ditches that carried the precious liquid to properties throughout the city and beyond. Virginia loved walking with her dad up 31st

Avenue to Buckeye Road that was also US 80, a ribbon of concrete where cars raced in opposite directions divided only by a painted line. At this corner, stood a row of mailboxes accompanied by a large wooden electrical pole. Attached to the pole was a nine-inch by twelve-inch covered wooden utility box. Harold reached inside the box to retrieve the water schedule and wrote the number of irrigation minutes he would need for the future week. He also made a mental note of the current week's schedule.

Often, the water flowed to their property during the nighttime hours. Many times Harold woke Virginia to help him with the irrigation. He knew she loved the adventure of traipsing through other people's yards and climbing fences when someone had neglected to pull their head gates and allow the water to flow down to the next property. This was a fun time for her. Eventually, they would locate the culprit who had fallen asleep or maybe tried to gain a few extra minutes of watering time. They would pull the gates and follow the water back home.

Harold and Virginia directed the water over

the land to quench the orchard where plums, apricots, pomegranates, and figs grew. Harold talked about how the new pecan trees required extra attention. When he revealed the number of years it would take for the saplings to actually produce nuts, Virginia thought him to be a pure optimist. He told stories, allowed her climbs up the fig tree to observe the water flowing underneath, and watched her eat the luscious fruit. They guided the water toward Ruth's emerging rose garden. Fragrant gardenias and American Beauty roses lined the perimeter of the house along with a hedgerow and vines that clung to the stucco. Virginia loved the heady scents of perfume that filled the house when the windows were opened. Finally, they watered the Japanese Privet that distinguished the outside edge of the property. Harold planted it to form a privacy hedge and dust screen from the dirt road. They avoided flooding the small fishpond in front, opened the headgates when their time was complete, and contentedly went back to bed.

Virginia felt all of the love and security a little girl could want, but there was something else her parents wanted to provide. Harold and Ruth, especially Ruth, set out with determination to share with little Virginia the thing they both sought in their younger years -- opportunity. They insisted on music, dance, and educational instruction to enhance her life experiences.

The accordion boasted popularity among instruments at the time, and Virginia began lessons at age five. Ruth insisted on keeping a daily practice schedule. Virginia didn't mind playing, the accordion was fun and she enjoyed making music.

Willard Trick started Virginia off on the squeezebox and soon the talented pre-schooler was ready for the stage! She joined Roberta Bragdon's select Tiny Tots, a variety group that performed at multiple functions and events throughout the city. The little crowd pleasers sang, danced, performed acrobatics, and bowed to thunderous applause. Ruth sewed Virginia a beautiful costume and soon she was ready for her first public performance. She took the stage at the historic Adams Hotel and played her twelve-base Horner for a crowd that included Arizona's governor, Sidney P. Osborn.

Ruth's insistence that Virginia practice paid off with multiple invitations to perform beginning with the Tiny Tots. Virginia shined during performances throughout the capitol city. She played on KOY radio as Jack Williams announced and Roberta Bragdon played piano accompaniment. Howard Pyle, on radio station KTAR, invited Virginia to his show as well. These early entertainment contacts became long-time friends of little Virginia.

Virginia was as talented off stage as she was on. She related well to adults and easily formed relationships with the mayor, city council members, and town merchants; both Jack Williams and Howard Pyle later served as governors of Arizona. Virginia grew up surrounded by the leaders of her community, city, and state. The family of the automotive painter developed friendships with business owners, politicians, their doctor, and dentist in a place where there seemed to be few social barriers, especially for talented little girls with Shirley Temple curls.

Time for Virginia to attend school drew near along with the anticipation of a new member to the Howell family. Little Mickey brought the baby crib back to life with his smiles and coos and, of course, the occasional loud, unmistakable signal that he needed something. Mickey received Ruth's abundant love and attention while Virginia learned all of what first grade had to offer. When Virginia came home from school, Mickey was the perfect little cuddly bundle to play with and a great audience for accordion practice.

Virginia walked either one-fourth mile to the bus stop or one mile on to school, something she was accustomed to because Ruth never drove. After gaining a little experience navigating her way to and from school independently, she was entrusted with going into town to pay the utility bills. Virginia rode the bus into Phoenix and then walked through downtown with bills and checks clasped tightly in her hands. She enjoyed her excursions and made extra stops along the way to visit people she knew. Newberry's five and dime store sat at the corner of Washington and First Avenue. Virginia went in to say hello to the clerks, to listen to Hazel playing the latest music on the piano, and also to look over the new toys and trinkets. Sometimes she went to the doctor's office to visit with Irma, the nurse and receptionist, sometimes the dentist's office received a call. Virginia knew them from her occasional health care visits, but mostly due to regular attendance at the First United Methodist Church in downtown Phoenix.

Some of her school teachers also attended the same church. Virginia liked all of her teachers and often visited with them in their homes, at church, and on visits back to former classrooms. By the sixth grade, Virginia believed she was ready to take on a teaching position of her own. Bill Henderson lived half a mile from her home and wanted to learn to play accordion. Virginia, a skilled performer on the instrument, accepted her first teaching job and began walking to the small frame house on Pima Street once each week. She waited for her knock to be answered on the front stoop, which was just big enough to receive guests. Mr. Henderson's Seeing Eye dog greeted her with skepticism. The German Shepherd had a mouth the size of Virginia's face. The dog wore a harness with a handle extending up to Mr. Henderson's hand and took the job of protecting her master seriously. The first few weeks of lessons consisted of gaining the trust of the dog so Virginia could eventually place Mr. Henderson's hands on the keys properly.

Virginia discovered Mr. Henderson's ear for music and her own passion for teaching. She looked forward to her time spent with Mr. Henderson in the sparsely furnished front room. He anticipated his lessons as well and prepared for Virginia's arrival by moving a wooden chair from the dining table into the front room. She counted to keep time while he learned to play Silent Night and other songs he enjoyed.

From her earliest memories and throughout her life, Virginia loved people. She loved meeting new people. She loved staying in touch with people she already knew. Her vivaciousness and kindness drew people to her; and she embraced them no matter their age, gender, or abilities. She instinctively saw past an individual's obstacles to their abilities and believed even a blind man could play accordion.

Growth and Opportunity

In the early 1900s, Arizona boasted a thriving economy led by industries of the five C's: cattle, cotton, copper, citrus, and climate. However, major droughts damaged the cattle and citrus industries and the Great Depression handicapped what was left. Hot wind blew through rural ghost towns throughout the state when residents abandoned their property in hopes of finding prosperity, or simply a meal, elsewhere.

Arizona's decline continued until government officials authorized the military to begin building training bases in the state. US armed services united in preparation to enter World War II. It was time for the military, also weakened by the depression, to regain its strength and size to face off against hostile world aggressors. Eager to take advantage of Arizona's cheap labor, low taxes, unoccupied land, and good railroads, construction of an airfield or a military base took only weeks to complete. Soon more than a dozen such installments sprung up around Phoenix and Tucson. Flight training soared through the state's clear skies. Manufacturing plants were not far behind. Consolidated Aircraft, AiResearch, Goodyear Aircraft Corporation, Alcoa, Inc., and Allison Steel Company hustled into production to supply the military with needed equipment and parts.

Harold participated in the war effort by accepting a job at Goodyear Aircraft Corporation. He, and many others, assembled parts for combat aircraft. Working for Goodyear came with some privileges, such as taking his family on a flight in the Goodyear Blimp out of Litchfield Park. To prepare for the special occasion, Ruth put on her Sunday best. She double checked Virginia's appearance and had little Mickey looking dapper.

Before wartime changed priorities, Goodyear Blimps served in a promotional capacity. The huge aircraft teamed up with celebrities for movie promotions, thrilled and surprised onlookers by landing on top of department store buildings, and even soared through the air with a trapeze stunt artist dangling below performing tricks and flips.

World War II insisted the fun times became more focused and the Navy commissioned Goodyear to use blimp technology to build flying aircraft carriers. The challenge resulted in a behemoth aircraft that spanned the length of two and a half football fields, carried ninety-one crewmembers, and became a base for scouting planes. The planes "landed" by carefully latching a hook located on the top of the plane's frame onto a type of ladder that lowered from the belly of the blimp. Once the two aircrafts connected, the blimp's ladder raised back inside delivering pilot and plane for refueling and debriefing within the flying air base.

The opportunity to ride on a blimp was rare and unforgettable. The Howell family seized the chance and relished every aspect of the experience. The special day stood in contrast to Ruth's life back on her family's Nebraska farm. Life on the farm certainly would not have involved high-flying excursions. Ruth did not fulfill her dream of graduating high school and pursuing a medical degree, but the grandness of the blimp perfectly illustrated the soaring opportunities she wanted to provide for her own children.

Ruth wasn't the only person looking for opportunity. Thousands of families came to Phoenix for jobs at the new military bases and manufacturing facilities. The city exploded with hustle, bustle, and increasing prosperity. Many of the enlisted men who were assigned to the area for boot camp liked it enough to return to Phoenix after the war. They observed climate advantages, job opportunity, and a good family atmosphere.

Only the growing numbers of the student body at Phoenix Union High School matched the city's climbing population. The state's largest high school, PUHS was serious about preparing graduates for life. Students chose a field of study ranging from business to liberal arts or pre-medical to secretarial. Clubs and organizations on campus reflected a wide range of interests and supplied many opportunities to gain experience in leadership, organization, and productivity.

Phoenix Union was a small city of its own.

A teaching position at the large school earned a higher salary than many colleges offered professors. Only the very best educators were awarded jobs at PUHS. Many members of the faculty held PhD's in their fields. The education standards and expectations were high and students rose to the challenge.

By the time Virginia entered high school, the fifth and final member of the Howell family, Patricia, was three years old. In spite of the twelve years difference in the girls' ages, they were the best of friends. Patricia spent a lot of time with her big sister and wanted to do everything Virginia did. Patricia learned music and practiced twirling a baton alongside her role model.

Occasionally, Mickey, joined his sisters on stage playing the trumpet or accordion. The Howell trio shared their talents disrupting monotony for the inmates at the Arizona State Prison at Florence, bringing joy to nursing home residents, entertaining their peers at church programs, even accepting invitations to perform at some of Phoenix's black churches.

Dixie Yost taught Virginia piano which the

young girl studied seriously. Ruth continued to place a high priority on practice and the Howell house seemed to always be filled with music of some sort. Virginia was skilled enough to play the passionate Prelude in C Sharp Minor by Rachmaninov for her eighth grade recital at the Phoenix Women's Club.

As soon as she received her driver's license, Virginia was ready to pursue her passion for teaching. Her Saturdays consisted of driving all over Phoenix to teach piano to students young and old. Virginia took her teaching very seriously and expected her students to do the same. They learned scales and classical style as well as chords so they could play popular music and entertain. Mimicking her mother's style of accountability, Virginia left her students with assignments to practice throughout the week and expected them to know the pieces when she returned.

Virginia's musical talent drew her to the high school's marching band where she added the clarinet to her musical resume. Her twirling performance, along with Patricia -- her adorable, pre-school sidekick, soon secured a half-time feature spotlight for the Howell sisters. The shimmering satin and sparkling sequins of the matching costumes dazzled onlookers. A large tassel highlighted each of the short, white boots sitting far below the skirts. Nothing was more popular on Friday nights than PUHS football. Due to Virginia's halftime performances, she soon became known and recognized by nearly everyone at the large school.

It was within the confines of the sprawling PUHS campus that Virginia eventually met five, loosely-connected girls. One day they would become tightly interwoven and fill a special role throughout the rest of their lives.

The Girls of Dami Phi Datum

Snookie's birth certificate read Leon Ora Lintz. While her parents awaited her arrival, her father brokered a deal with her mother that he would have the honor and privilege of naming the baby. Without hesitation he chose Leon Ora.

Born and raised on a Kansas farm, Leon's father had chores from sun up until sun down. No strangers to tough times and hard work, he and his brother enlisted in the Army at the ages of sixteen and seventeen. The brothers' journey with the Army took them to France where they each drove an ambulance during World War I. After Armistice, the Santa Leonora brought them home, and a few years later, Leon bore the name of the homecoming steamship.

From the moment Leon Ora's father laid eyes on her, he called her Snookie. He got his wish to name her but never used her given name. Other people did. Beginning in kindergarten, the first day of school roll call routine began. Teachers called out names seamlessly until reaching the letter L in the alphabet. Leon Lintz. Matching the face with the name always led to a pause and a question about why a girl was named Leon. She grew up telling the story of the Santa Leonora and always referred to the ship as the Leon Ora as her father remembered it.

Snookie was only four years old when her mother died. By the time she reached high school, her stepmother had also passed. Her alcoholic father functioned well enough to maintain their small apartment and booze in the fridge, with much help from Leon, of course. Love and family support were foreign concepts to her. That's when she and Martha Martin began walking to school together.

They lived near each other, and the city bus stopped right on the corner. When the weather was nice, which included most days in Phoenix, the friends walked the three miles to school. They enjoyed walking and the time for lighthearted banter before the seriousness of school began. During these walks with Martha, Snookie learned to laugh. Martha shared with her the gift of joy and the pleasure of uncontrollable laughter. For the first time in her life, Snookie laughed until her sides hurt. They laughed until they were out of breath and so weak in the knees they stopped to roll in the grass and laugh some more. Snookie reveled in the silliness and uncontrollable giggles.

Like Snookie, Martha came from a single-parent home. She lived with her mother and sister. Her petite frame played disguise to her energy and strength, but nothing could hide her silly sense of humor.

Mr. Wilson taught geology at PUHS. He arranged the tables and chairs in the room into multiple rows of a horseshoe pattern. He liked to walk inside the horseshoe as he lectured so he could easily see the faces of all students. Mr. Wilson's seating chart placed Barbara Witten directly across from Mary Lou Henson. The two girls didn't know each other, but Mary Lou set out to change that when she discovered one of the cutest boys in the class, Jim Witten, happened to be Barbara's cousin.

Jim often wore unique sweaters with designs knitted into them. Mary Lou approached Barbara and feigned interest in the sweaters to strike up a conversation. The two girls hit it off and quickly became fast friends who dubbed each other Lulu and Baba. Barbara introduced Mary Lou to her cousin Jim. They hit it off as well.

Mary Lou's inquiry about the sweaters was not only to meet Barbara and Jim; she truly had a great interest in fashion. Mary Lou, an excellent seamstress, sewed beautiful, fashionable, and perfectly-tailored outfits. Growing up as the oldest of three children in a working-class family, Mary Lou wisely used the money she had to invest in things she couldn't make. She wore the popular silver and turquoise, Indian-crafted Concho belt and a squash blossom necklace with the clothes she made herself.

Shirley Johnson grew up on Seventeenth Avenue, catty corner from the state capitol building. Her father ran the bar for the Phoenix Labor Temple. Whenever the union gathered for a meeting, he opened the bar and sold beer to the members. Her family lived in the apartment behind the bar.

As Shirley reached her teenage years, she decided to work toward acquiring the things she wanted in life. Mostly, she wanted friends. As a child, she knew some of the other kids were not allowed to come play at her house because of the proximity to the bar. A girl four years Shirley's senior advised her to join as many clubs and organizations as possible when she entered high school and promised a full life would result. Shirley also wanted the attention and companionship of a good, dependable man. Shirley's father had passed away when she was young and she missed out on sharing many experiences with him. Finally, she wanted a large family to fill the table at dinnertime. Growing up as an only child, she longed for dinner-time companionship and conversation instead of her many nights of eating from a TV tray.

Shirley took the advice of her friend and became involved in extracurricular activities at PUHS. The announcement of a newly initiated pompon squad piqued Shirley's interest and she prepared to audition. Miss Sally Young, a new teacher, volunteered to sponsor the dance team and held the girls to high standards. The pioneering group worked hard to prove themselves. They practiced two to three hours after school every day! Miss Young led the girls to be truly professional in their performances. She also instilled in them the responsibility to be good examples to the student body and honorable ambassadors of the school. The pompon girls soon developed a reputation of girls with high principles who were fabulous performers.

The description of the pompon girls fit Virginia perfectly! Willing to hang up her baton to join the high-kicking troop, Virginia signed up for auditions as well. However, band director Harvey Zorn, was a member of the judging panel. Seeing the highlight of his halftime show trying out for another squad horrified him. His forceful "no" vote kept Virginia and her little sister Patricia as twirling halftime highlights for his marching band.

Soon Virginia would become an important member of this group, just not the way she expected.

The Dami Phi Datum Charter

Bob Cannon wore number forty-five for the PUHS Coyotes football team and combed his dark, straight hair over to one side. Taking his helmet on and off often caused a stray lock to sweep across his forehead. He used his slightly disheveled look and boyish smile to attract Shirley's attention. Shirley Johnson was one of the prettiest girls in the junior class who did not miss the fact that Bob carried himself with the swagger of a high school senior playing on the state's class A championship team. This cockiness intrigued Shirley while simultaneously frustrating her.

In spite of their differences, the pompon girl dated the football star. Bob rushed for yardage in their relationship while Shirley threw penalty flags. The scoreboard ticked up and down as unpredictably as the stock market. Bob and Shirley had independent ideas that were not always in sync. These differences led to arguments. One argument became the tipping point for Shirley and launched her into action to make some serious modifications.

Shirley took assessment of her life and realized her quest for friendships had opened her up to some negative influences. She needed to surround herself with quality relationships that would encourage her personal growth. Besides that, she was really angry with Bob!

Shirley took her bruised heart to her best friends on the pompon squad, Snookie and Barbara. She outlined the situation with Bob and shared her decision to move away from some of the bad influences in her life. Snookie and Barbara were tasked with recruiting good, positive new friends for Shirley. Barbara brought Mary Lou into the group and Snookie asked her friend Martha to join them. Everyone knew Virginia as the majorette who led the marching band and stood in the half-time spotlight.

Shirley hosted an impromptu initiation party while her mother was out of town. It included a ride through the city in her mom's 1939 Chevy Business Coupe. One bench seat stretched across the front with carpeted storage space behind. Shirley piled as many girls as she could into the front seat. The girl sitting next to her straddled the stick shift while she drove. Not wanting to waste any space, two, sometimes three more girls squeezed into the storage space behind the seat.

After racing through town, the girls focused on the business at hand. They rallied around Shirley and confirmed her sentiment that boys were indeed immature, frustrating, irritating, and not entirely worth their valuable time. After all, it was nearly the 1950's and these girls had dreams for a future that involved education and careers. Studying hard and making good grades sat near the top of their priority lists. Refusing to be deterred from their goals by the lure of relationships, they formed a pact, a girls club. Swearing off boys, the club charter stated each girl could date merely once each month. They named the newly formed group Dami Phi Datum.

Shirley had spent the previous summer in Sioux City, Iowa where she was introduced to sororities. She thought her clever play on the

Greek alphabet for the club's name spoke of maturity beyond their years and stood as a defiant insult to Bob. It was perfect! Snookie told a male friend from school about the group. When she revealed the name, his expression became quizzical then challenging. He declared, "Well, hell if we care!"

Shirley's impetuousness initiated new friendships among the selected group of girls who initially shared a strong moral compass and honorable character traits. Those qualities held them together long enough to deepen bonds to each other until true friendship developed.

The girls kept a busy calendar without needing to fill it with dates. In addition to school studies, they stayed after school for practice to prepare for all of their performances. The pompon squad danced wearing white, form-fitting costumes made from corduroy fabric. The small waist gave way to a full skirt that extended only to mid-thigh. Kicks and spins revealed a red satin lining and matching satin shorts. The turtleneck and long sleeves helped maintain modesty. The popular troop entertained not only the huge crowds of thousands at football games, but also civic events around Phoenix and on the train platform when dignitaries arrived into town. Virginia, twirling her baton dressed in showy satin and sequins, performed at many of the same events.

Martha never tried out for the pompon squad. Dancing and cheering did not interest her personally, but she was a good friend to Snookie and waited through practices to walk home together. Martha enjoyed hanging out with the pompon girls and helped with administrative tasks or errands whenever she could. She dubbed herself the pompon mascot.

The Dami Phi girls were beautiful. They sported the popular hairstyle of short bangs curled across their foreheads. The crown and sides smoothed only to give way to more curls framing their faces. Virginia's heavy brown hair made the style easy for her to maintain. Everyday school attire consisted of looking their best in skirts and blouses accompanied by highly shined saddle oxfords or ballerina slippers. Keeping up with fashion and hairstyles, school studies, and after school practices rounded out a full life for the Dami Phi girls and made the rules of the club's charter fairly easy to follow. No boys!

The regulations held firm for a full two months! Then, Shirley and Bob patched things up. In an expected turn of events, Shirley declared the Dami Phis were allowed to date once a week.

Not everyone took advantage of the new club dating policy, and the pledge bonding the girls together did not deter the boys from exerting efforts to be noticed. Frustration bubbled to the surface when the girls hardly detected the boys' hard work. One young man, Eugene Fuller, tried his best to gain Mary Lou's consideration. He made his disappointment known when he signed her yearbook, "To a very, very pretty little girl whose middle name should be Iceberg." Mary Lou gladly accepted the compliment!

On weekends the girls liked to pile into either Shirley's or Barbara's old Chevy cars. Everyone pitched in a nickel for gas, which cost twenty-five cents a gallon. Gassed up and ready to go, they drove to South Mountain for picnics, the Polar Bar drive-in restaurant, movies, ball games, or wherever they would find lots of friends hanging out. At the drive-in restaurant, a carhop ran out to meet the car and hopped onto the running board to begin taking their order before they even came to a full stop. The carhop always told the girls about the Zombie Special, a huge ice cream concoction that cost a dollar! The girls kept a careful eye on their budget and ordered five-cent Cokes and ten-cent French fries instead.

One night Mary Lou was the last to be delivered home. Her instructions to Baba were, "Home James!" Upon reaching Lulu's house, instead of stopping to let Mary Lou out at the curb, Barbara simply drove over the curb across the front lawn and stopped the Chevy right beside the front steps. The following morning, Mary Lou's mother was heard to exclaim, "Someone drove across our yard. Look at those tracks!" Mary Lou silently retreated to her room as a sly smile overtook her face.

Bob seemed to like that Shirley spent time

with her good friends. Going to dances when everyone had a date and sometimes hanging out as a group was fun. Eventually, even the staunchest Dami Phi girls began to consider the idea of sharing their hearts with a worthy suitor. The friends grew closer as they shared school and fun times together.

Dami Phi News, Volume I, August 31, 1949

Cheeky wit and mischievousness spilled out of Martha. She used her talents to produce a club newsletter. The smudged ink of a mimeograph machine churned out copies for the exclusive list of subscribers. Although the publication became an immediate hit with its readership, the second edition waited exactly thirty-two years to follow.

The Dami Phi News, Volume I, published August 31, 1949 noted Martha Martin as Editor, Martha Martin as Business Manager, Martha Martin as Reporter, and Martha Martin as Publisher. The First Edition Of A World Famous Paper led with ...

"PAPER HAS EIGHT SUBSCRIBERS."

Phoenix, Aug. 31-Today the first edition of the "Dami Phi News" came off the press. The purpose of this paper is to build up the Dami Phi

Datum Club treasury. Each month a copy will be sold at five cents to each member. It is believed that the members will enjoy the paper and contribute material to it. This first edition is a trial copy and it is hoped that everyone will give comment on it.

The paper is designed to tell of Dami Phi happenings and to inform the Dami Phi's on outside information. So if you have any jokes, gossip, stories or any other material, please put it in the "Dami Phi News" by calling 96396 and asking for the editor, Martha Martin.

The Dami Phis have a fine club supported by their eight members: Joyce Berutti, 2006 West Washington; Zel Ellenbaum, 3016 North 17th Avenue; Mary Lou Henson, 1822 East Willetta; Virginia Howell, 1302 South 31st Avenue; Shirley Johnson, 1637 West Jefferson; Leon Lintz, 1601 West Roosevelt; Martha Martin, 1301 West Lathan; Barbara Witten, 1305 East Granada Road.

If you have any "Letters To The Editor" address them to 1301 W. Latham and they will be published in the next edition of "Dami Phi News."

THE END ****

Once Martha took care of business, she wrote about topics of real concern to her subscribers.

IT COULD HAPPEN TO ANYONE

Screwie Berutti
Zinky Ellenbaum
Measly Henson
Wow Howell
Jerk Johnson
Chintzey Lintz
Moron Martin
Burb Witten

What do you think? Do you believe these names fit better than their real names? I do.

HENSON HAS HARD LIFE!

POOR, poor Mary Lou Henson, known to some as Lu Lu. As editor of this great paper, I believe it is only proper that I tell you about the hard life Mary Lou has led. Each one of these incidents is a true hardship so please be sympathetic with her.

One of Mary Lou's first misfortunes, when she was younger she was playing around in her back yard and her telephone rang. She was running across the yard to answer it when she stepped on a needle. The needle was upright, sticking out of the ground and she ran the whole needle up into her foot. Her mother had to pull it out with the pliers.

Another time she was skating and the front wheel of her skate came off and she fell and cut her head on a palm tree.

Once Mary Lou went to a girlfriend's house when she was about thirteen. She and her girlfriend were in her girlfriend's backyard playing in ankle deep water. There was a flood light there also which was connected to the swing. The floodlight had a short circuit and when poor Mary Lou touched the steel part of the swing her hair stood up, she couldn't scream, or let go. They turned the flood light off and she fainted for a few seconds.

When Lu Lu was in the eighth grade she was a great softball player. One day she was pitching and Sara Wier was playing first base when someone hit a fly ball. Lu Lu and Sara both tried for it and ran into each other. Lu Lu knocked Sara's front tooth, and Sara cut Lu Lu above her right eye. Lu Lu was in the hospital about 45 minutes and had to have 7 stitches taken in her head.

These are only a few of the hardships of poor, poor Mary Lou.

TALENT IN THE CLUB

This club also has talent along with nonsense.

Joyce plays the radio
Zel plays the phonograph
Mary Lou the piano
Virginia the piano, and an accordion
Shirley plays the piano, dances, and sings
Leon sews nicely
Martha acts silly and plays the piano
Barbara plays the piano and accordion

HEAD LIGHTS AND TAIL LIGHTS!!!!

Mother: Don't you get John and Mike mixed up?

Daughter: Sure, I get John mixed up one night and Mike the next.

* * *

Father: Is there anything worse than being old and bent?

Son: Yes, being young and broke.

* * *

1st Person: If there were four men in a life-boat and they had three cigarettes and no way to light them, what would they do?

2nd Person: I don't know.

1st Person: They would throw one cigarette away and then the boat would be one cigarette lighter!

The Whistler –
I bought a wooden whistle,
But it wooden whistle.
I bought a steel whistle,
But steel it wooden whistle.
I bought a lead whistle,

But steel they wooden lead me whistle.
I bought a tin whistle,
And now I tin whistle.

??? DID YOU KNOW ???

Barbara Whitten had her first date with Garvin Cuntz when she was a sophomore?

Leon Lintz had her first date with Bob Kelly and they went to a dance at P.U.H.S.?

Martha Martin had her first date with Monty Hough and they went to the show, that was the year after the seventh grade?

Leon Lintz had her first date with Gene Brown on April 29, 1949?

JOYce Berutti doesn't like to have a "smack" kiss?

Barbara Witten can wiggle her ears?

Leon Lintz was named for a ship by the name of Leon Ora?

Johnny Houghten has a crush on Judy Grims? While Pat DeMour has a crush on Johnny?

Shirley Johnson got ran over when she was four and got her leg broken?

Mary Lou Henson's mother didn't have any reason for naming Mary Lou, MARY LOU?

Barbara Witten went to six different schools and plans to attend Tempe next year?

Martha Martin put a dent in her mother's new Studebaker car?

That Zel Ellenbaum's address is 315 4th Street, North Staples, Minn.?

The newsletter sparked giggles and whispers among the club members. Never taking themselves too seriously, the girls joked and laughed together for hours. Martha's plans for a monthly newsletter fizzled, but the friendships grew in volumes.

From Dami Phi Datum to Don't Mindi Phi Du

Although the agreement to avoid dating prevailed, the girls seemed to waste no time marrying after high school. Snookie, Martha, Shirley, and Barbara were seniors when Bob and his teammate Gene Brown left for The University of Arizona on football scholarships. Bob kissed Shirley goodbye; Gene said so long to Snookie and the boys became Wildcats in Tucson, Arizona, a long three-hour drive away.

Gene had worn number fifty-five for the PUHS football team alongside Bob. Gene's big smile gave away his secret mischievous ideas and endeared him to his fellow students. His leadership skills were put to good use on the football field as well as serving as class president for both his junior and senior years. His high school involvement set the stage for a few dates with Snookie the year before he left for college.

When Gene went to the University of Arizona, they didn't try to maintain a long distance relationship. Gene dated a few coeds on campus and soon realized Snookie outshined them all. Before the end of his freshman year, Gene asked Snookie to go steady.

Bob and Shirley put more effort into shortening the three-hour drive that separated Tucson and Phoenix and kept their unpredictable relationship going. The couple soon became engaged and maintained a steady flow of letters to keep in touch between personal visits. A telephone call was long distance, expensive, and happened only on special occasions.

Shirley graduated PUHS in May and walked down the aisle to meet Bob in July. Gene and Snookie had the same plan, but moved a little more slowly. An engagement ring was Snookie's high school graduation gift from Gene. They married the following spring.

Holding true to the Dami Phi Datum pledge, Barbara and Martha proudly graduated PUHS without any romantic entanglements. Martha joined many of her classmates at the University of Arizona at Tucson where she dashed the dreams of her mother by deciding not to pledge a sorority. Instead, she forged her own path and pursued a degree in teaching with an emphasis in physical education. Within four years she graduated with a BA and took a job teaching P.E. in San Diego, California.

Barbara, taking her pompon skills to Arizona State College at Tempe, stayed closer to home. ASC during this time was battling for the title of university. School enrollment tripled when military personnel returned to the Arizona sunshine to take advantage of GI Bill dollars to further their education. The school's expansion of classes and programs led to a proposal for the college to be recognized as a university. Rival University of Arizona graduates, who dominated the Board of Regents and held positions in the state legislature, protested the change with determination. Students signed petitions while state officials buried the proposal in committees. Students began using the name university as a sort of rebellion, and The Arizona Republic even took the stance of referring to the school as university, declaring it a matter of accuracy in journalism.

The stalemate ended when Governor Howard Pyle cast the deciding vote at the Board of Regents meeting to accept recommendations for Arizona State to hold the title, university. Yes, this was the same Howard Pyle, formerly of KTAR radio in Phoenix, who sometimes brought Virginia in as a guest on his program.

One of many students to adopt the university name long before it became official, Barbara displayed her school pride through her diligent studies and as a part of the pompon squad. She used her experience from PUHS to help organize Arizona State's first pom squad to dance for the Sun Devils.

A handsome Navy man, attending classes with the help of the GI Bill, managed to catch Barbara's attention in spite of the demand of her classes and extracurricular activities. Gene Smith sat across the room in one of her classes held in historic Old Main, the original building erected on campus in 1885. Barbara knew he was "the one" almost immediately. Perhaps his introduction to the class is what endeared him to her. When the professor asked each student to introduce him/herself, with a perplexed expression, Gene said, "My name is Gene Smith, and I think that I am in the wrong class."

A mutual friend, Daisy Yee, facilitated personal introductions, and Gene and Barbara quickly became a couple. The duo dated the remainder of the school calendar and married at the launch of Barbara's sophomore year.

While the older Dami Phis entered the college years, Mary Lou and Virginia used their talents to spur on the PUHS Coyotes. After winning the state championship the year before, the green, up-and-coming players heard bleak predictions. Fans cheered the underdogs to a winning season and held their seats for the fabulous half time performances. Virginia and little Patricia, now an elementary student, marched and twirled together every Friday night in front of the packed Montgomery Stadium and other stadiums throughout the state. Ruth outdid herself on tailoring the white satin uniforms, which were even more elaborate than previous seasons. The red sequined hem of the circle skirts rose well above mid-thigh. Red tasseled shoulder epaulettes topped off the sequined bodice that rose to a high collar with intricate trim around the neck. Ruth knew the flashy costumes could not outshine the talent of her daughters' performances but fully unleashed her tailoring abilities. Virginia and Patricia put in many hours of practice to execute the routines perfectly.

Ruth's continued encouragement for her children to be involved in a myriad of experiences gave Virginia quite a lengthy high school resume. All four years at PUHS, she was a featured accordion soloist in the acclaimed Les Follies directed by Lois Holliday and backed by the Orly Illes' orchestra. Her senior year, Joan Burr joined Virginia for a duet, playing Rhapsody in Blue. The two girls played near identical Delape' accordions that Willard Trick, Virginia's first accordion teacher, brought home from Italy when he returned from WWII. The crowd erupted in applause in response to the performance.

The annual Turkey Day game between rivals Phoenix Union and North High was the biggest game in the Valley of the Sun. Virginia and Patricia invested extra effort into the single game that seemed to capture all of the city of Phoenix. Soon after the big game, PUHS selected its first Salad Bowl princess. Each area school sent their princess candidate to ride in the Salad Bowl Parade on New Year's Day. Fellow Dami Phi club member, Shirley had represented PUHS as Salad Bowl princess in 1950, and 1951, Virginia was one of the four finalists.

Virginia put her other talents to good use as well. Her organizational abilities and creative use of adjectives earned a reputation and a lead spot, along with Mary Lou Brion, heading the prestigious PUHS yearbook staff. Their 1951, Phoenician yearbook earned All-American honors for its content and production while Virginia maintained scholarship level academic accomplishments, as well as first-chair in the concert band's clarinet section.

The long practices, hours of work, and time devoted to studies brought Virginia joy as did relationships and friendships. Virginia knew a lot people at school and around town, but many more knew her. She was known and respected wherever she went. She easily connected with a variety of people on multiple levels. It's no surprise this attractive, confident young lady mesmerized a certain Air Force pilot at Williams Air Force Base near Chandler.

The early seeds of romance began when Beverly Wisenhoefer moved to Phoenix. Beverly's life stood in stark contrast to Virginia's. Growing up a military brat, Beverly had no roots or a single place called home. Accustomed to finding her way in new schools, Beverly easily made friends with Virginia when her family moved to Arizona.

Her father had retired after thirty years of service and chose Phoenix as the best place to settle down. The warm sunshine, strong economy, and significant military presence created an attractive advertisement for relocation to the Valley of the Sun.

Beverly's mother had more difficulty adjusting to civilian life. Frequent trips to Williams Air Force Base kept her connected to the military lifestyle she knew best. She enjoyed shopping in the commissary and playing bridge at the Officer's Club on Fridays. Beverly's mother enjoyed having drinks at bridge and sometimes brought Beverly along to drive her home. While her mother played cards, Beverly attended dances at the Cadet Club. As soon as football and marching band season ended, Beverly persuaded Virginia to come along.

Virginia loved to dance, and Beverly convinced her easily. Virginia's first Cadet Club appearance was January 6, 1951. The festive atmosphere reflected some of the formality and discipline of a military base mixed with a strong dose of revelry from a group of men who seemed to have a knack for losing privileges of leave. After several months of being confined to base, they warmly welcomed outsiders, especially beautiful ones.

Virginia enjoyed the good-spirited atmosphere, and a surprising wealth of cultural diversity. The base's international defense training program included allied pilots from both France and Holland. Handsome young men with fabulous accents learned advanced jet-flying techniques alongside Americans at Williams AFB.

Dancing with a Dutch pilot, Virginia focused all of her attention on interpreting his tilted English when a very self-assured young man interrupted the couple. Audrey D. Hare introduced himself as his pilot's call sign, "Rabbit." The twenty-three year old Navy veteran of World War II did his best to monopolize Virginia's time the rest of the evening. Before the two were forced to part ways, Rabbit stated matter-of-factly he planned to marry Virginia. She did little to contain her laughter at his absurd statement. Months passed before Virginia learned what Rabbit's friends already knew: what Rabbit says, Rabbit does.

Harold, Ruth, and Virginia, in one of the professional portraits that were so important to Ruth, 1937.

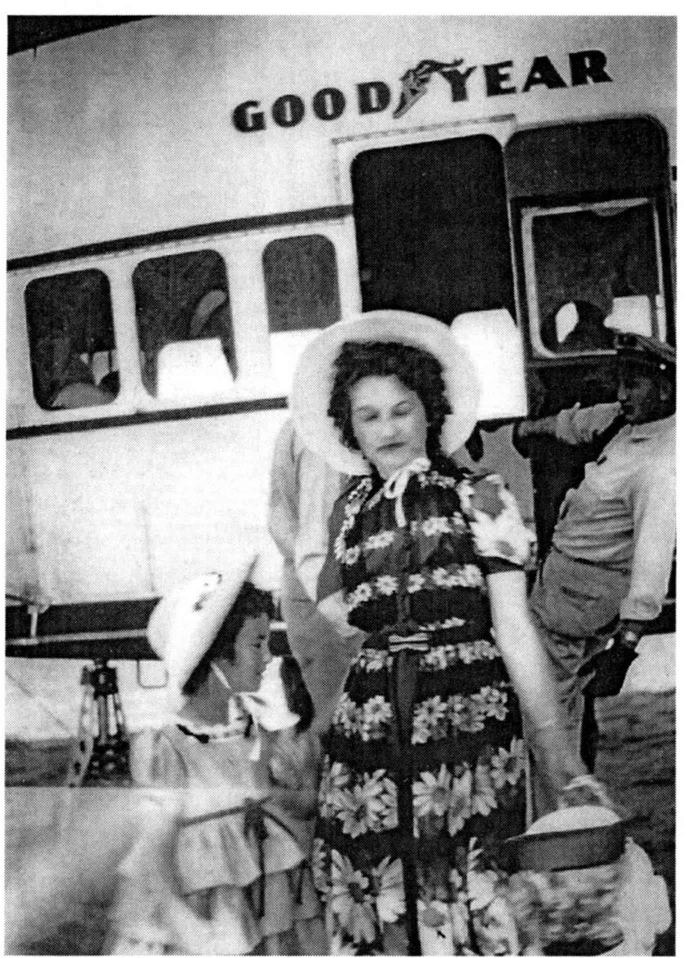

Virginia, Ruth and Mickey prepare to board the blimp and experience flying for the first time.

Mrs. Lillian Linsey leads the band to promote the sell of war bonds in downtown Phoenix at Central and Adams. The government spent twice as much during wartime as it had in its entire existence leading up to the war. President Roosevelt raised money by increasing taxes and the sale of massive amounts of war bonds. Mickey sits atop the cab on the left, Virginia takes center behind Mrs. Linsey, Joan Burr is to the right of Virginia, the rest of the band were Mrs. Linsey's grandchildren. Circa 1943.

Audrey Hare and Merlin Clark pose with their latest aircraft acquisition in 1948. After returning from World War II, Audrey pursued an aviation career while Merlin went to college.

Harold and his children are all dressed up and ready for Patricia's baptismal service at the First Methodist Church in Phoenix. Virginia is twelve years old, Mickey is six years old. Virginia's children also wore the heirloom baptismal dress.

Ruth sewed costumes with the same perfection she expected from her children in their endeavors.

The PUHS marching band with mascot Patricia leading the way and Virginia behind on Washington Street. Rodeo Parade through downtown Phoenix, March 1949. Photo Roosevelt Tang.

Patricia, the youngest majorette in all of PUHS history, shined and sparkled alongside Virginia, later as an Arizona state champion twirler, and attended college on a twirling scholarship at Northern Arizona University.

Virginia and Rabbit pose for a portrait just after Rabbit returned from Korea after flying 112 missions, Bryan, Texas, 1952.

Army troops and 302nd Squadron pilots gather in German woods after enduring another escape and evasion exercise planned and executed by Leif Bangsboll. Front row: Army, Jim Annos, Rabbit Hare, Ed O'Rourke, Army. Back row: Jim Harris, Army, Army, Army, Buck, Army, Leif Bangsboll, Army liaison officer with 302nd Squadron, Bo Ellis, maintenance officer, Joe Daly, Don Breedlove, John Zartman, Army, Roy Alldritt, Monk Everheardt.

Diagnosed as legally blind and without bifocal vision, glasses transformed 9-month-old Bunni's young life. The specialized optical manufacturer had never made glasses for a patient so young. The Hare's travelled to Houston each year for a new pair of the highly customized glasses.

The Hare family during the long, cold tour at Truax AFB, Madison, Wisconsin, 1961. Allan, 8 years, Rhonda, 5 years, Valerie, 4 years, Bunni, 9 years.

Virginia plays her custom made Delape' accordion in one of many performances while stationed around the world. Here in Laon, France 1959.

Virginia and Rabbit take the spotlight at the Beta Sigma Phi Valentine Sweetheart Dance at the Mid-Pacific Country Club, Kailua, Hawaii. Circa 1967.

The Hawaiian Hares in 1968 just before Rabbit left for Vietnam; Rabbit, Virginia, Bunni, Allan, Rhonda, and Valerie. Virginia couldn't convince the kids to wear shoes the entire five years of living in Kailua, Hawaii.

Tropical flowers at the Illikai Hotel with Virginia and Bernice Oshita, the RN who handled the many Hare family medical needs for five years at Kaneoke Marine Corp Air Station while the Hares lived in Kailua, Hawaii 1965-70. This photo taken on one of Virginia's return visits.

The Hare family in their Imp boat on Sweetwater Hollow, 1972. Every water-loving Hare was proficient with a pole, jug fishing, or trot lining and could catch and clean dinner.

Howell family reunion at Grand Lake, 1973. Front row: Skip, Chris and Patricia Heck, Virginia, Harold Howell, Allan Hare with Charlie, Betsy and Mickey Howell. Back row: Bunni Hare, Andrea Heck, Rhonda Hare, Ruth Howell, Valerie and Rabbit Hare.

Mother Ruth loved visiting Oklahoma and called the Hare's Grand Lake home paradise. Virginia and Ruth on Ruth's last visit to Oklahoma, 1978.

Rabbit in his beloved GlaStar, built with Virginia. Of course he decorated it with squadron insignias.

"Rabbit" Hare

Audrey Hare was born with ears tuned to the sound of propeller airplanes. Even as a toddler, the distant humming alerted him to scan the skies before his chubby finger shot into the air and a delighted smile overtook his face. By the age of twelve he spent his extra time guiding a broom across the expanse of concrete hangers at Amarillo's Municipal Airport. Pushing the broom got him close to the airplanes and pilots he loved. He worked in exchange for flying lessons, and soon skillfully navigated the West Texas skies enjoying a peace and freedom without comparison. Any money earned beyond flying lessons stayed squirreled away for the day he qualified to test for a private pilot's license.

On his sixteenth birthday, cake and candles had to wait. Audrey had a test to take! He passed easily and began negotiating an airplane owner partnership with his buddy Merlin Clark. Both boys only had eyes for the sky and barely gave a thought to obtaining a driver's license or a car.

Audrey and Merlin agreed on which airplane to purchase, a forty horsepower Taylorcraft two-seater. Each contributed two hundred dollars and began transporting any person or package that would help fund their passion. Next, Audrey set his sights on earning his commercial pilot's license. He achieved that goal and continued to spend as much time as possible in the air, perhaps imagining himself a fighter pilot as World War II raged on and captured daily news headlines. News of jets entering into the fighting effort sparked lively conversations among the pilots at the Municipal Airport.

After completing only one semester of his senior year at Amarillo High School, Audrey joined nearly every other male in the class of 1945 and enlisted in the Navy. The enthusiastic young men dedicated themselves to defend freedom and left for boot camp within days of their enlistment. The hallways and classrooms of Amarillo High felt vacant and quiet in their absence.

Audrey's eighteenth birthday was still three months away. His parents signed the age waiver that allowed him to go to boot camp ninety days before the draft would have taken him. Enlisting had some advantages over the draft. Most men drafted went into the Army and fought on the ground throughout Europe. The Navy only accepted enlisted men. Knowing you were fighting alongside someone who was there by choice increased your confidence in the man doing battle beside you.

Many of the classmates experienced the rigors of boot camp in San Diego together and soon officially became sailors. During their training, Germany surrendered to the allies in Europe, but the Japanese continued the fight in the Pacific. A good number of Audrey's classmates were assigned to the same ship. Each young man from Amarillo represented a piece of home. The connection brought comfort and created an easy camaraderie.

Audrey gained his sea legs and fought the Pacific war for several months. When it seemed there would be no end to battling the relentless Japanese, the United States dropped the atomic bomb on the enemy who refused to quit fighting.

Japan finally surrendered August 1945. Audrey and a few thousand more enlisted men were deposited at Pearl Harbor to finish out their tenure. Audrey was designated to work with the Military Police and partnered with a strapping six-foot-two sailor. The two men policed downtown Honolulu and its Chinatown red light district, an area with a history of both cooperation and tension between military and local law enforcement.

A year before Audrey's arrival, Hotel Street in Chinatown hosted a handful of unofficially regulated brothels. MPs joined forces with local vice squads to police the area, protect sailors from sexually transmitted diseases, and confine the prostitutes to the designated houses. Hawaii's governor shut down the establishments and women who continued in the trade now did so in secret. Sailors who once waited in lines that stretched down the street now needed to be discrete to avoid upsetting the working relationship between MPs and local police. Audrey and his partner drove a Jeep to patrol back alleys, side streets, and outside bars looking for sailors who may have needed some guidance to return to their barracks.

After a year in Hawaii, Audrey received an honorable discharge and returned to Amarillo where his high school diploma awaited him. He filed away the documentation of his education and eagerly returned to his true love -- flying. As long as he was in the air, Audrey didn't really care why. His flying business, Panhandle Air Express, included spraying and dusting crops, making deliveries and picking things up, and taking individuals where they wanted to go. He worked hard to build up a fleet of five airplanes and celebrated the day in May 1949 when he went to the bank to pay off the loan on four of them. He soaked in the satisfaction of full ownership for a glorious five days until a tornado hit Tradewinds Airport. The unpredictable nature of the twister demolished Audrey's four airplanes without touching the one still carrying a bank note.

This piece of very bad luck easily convinced Audrey he might prefer to fly someone else's airplanes. The Air Force's advanced jet fighter pilot program looked exciting, challenging, and financially stable. Audrey eagerly volunteered for service; however, the physical exam proved to be a bit more thorough than WWII's qualifications for soldiers. His medical assessment required the extraction of his wisdom teeth before entering the aviation cadet program at Goodfellow Air Force Base in San Angelo, Texas. Soon after his arrival at Goodfellow AFB, Audrey received the call sign "Rabbit" and rarely ever heard his first name after that. Rabbit completed the primary flying program in Texas and received orders to report to Williams AFB in Chandler, Arizona for advanced single-engine pilot training.

The Korean Conflict raged with Russia arming North Korea with MiG-15 fighter jets, worthy opponents against the US F-86. The North Korean pilots were no match for the well-trained US military in a dogfight, but they decimated US bombing formations. An international race to develop faster, more stable, more capable jets ensued.

Lockheed developed the T-33, a two-seater training jet, for pilots already qualified to operate propeller aircraft. The 1951 classes of Able, Bravo, Charley, and Dog were the first in the Air Force to receive pilot training in the T-33 jet. Rabbit joined a group of pilots in Class 51-Dog who possessed a certain knack for getting under the commander's skin. Major Carter followed every rule, written or implied. Every infraction received swift punishment, and privileges to leave the base were the first revoked. Rabbit's squad was so consistently irritating they were only allowed to leave base twice throughout the entire six months of training.

Soon the 51-Dog cadets began marching to the flight line keeping rhythm to the chant, "Carter's chaaaaain gang. We're Carter's chaaaaain gang." The loudly broadcast news of distaste for the Major seemed to instill pride in their leader. Major Carter observed the advancing group from his post with a smile of satisfaction spread across his face.

After meeting Virginia, Rabbit grew to anticipate her arrival every Friday evening. When he couldn't leave base, she brought a small piece of the outside world to him. Virginia enjoyed dancing with Rabbit most Friday nights. He loved watching the shape of her mouth change as her lips moved, but made little progress toward understanding the words coming out. The full extent of the vast expectations placed on Virginia's future by her mother's dreams seemed irrelevant as he cradled her small waist in his hand and guided her across the dance floor.

It seemed impossible for Rabbit to grasp that Ruth believed her beautiful, musically-gifted, honor-roll student would be crowned Miss Arizona on her way to completing an education degree at Arizona State College. She would then use her education and talent to help inspire the youth of America. Perhaps most importantly, her photograph would fill a special dedicated frame in the family home. The frame with cracked glass hung above the door in the back mudroom. The tradition was for the photo of the family's most recent college graduate to occupy the frame until replaced by the next family member to graduate. The honor awaited Virginia as the first born, and the frame hung ready to be filled with her college graduation photograph.

Rabbit, deaf to Virginia's future, focused on making her understand his own situation. Words spilled from his mouth straight onto the floor with the gravity of his chosen profession. Life expectancy hovered around age twenty-eight. No life insurance company sold a policy to men in such a high-risk occupation. Only the military offered life insurance to guys like him, and the pay out was minimal. Should Virginia decide to take a chance on Rabbit, she would likely be a young, penniless widow.

Rabbit's warning affected Virginia the same way her future plans influenced him; the sobering truth looked good on him. Reality made him seem braver, more courageous, more daring, more desirable.

Plans and Reality Collide

Virginia made her family proud by graduating high school with honors and scholarships. With plans already in place to attend Arizona State College in a few short months, she felt her future overflowed with promise and possibility.

Her Phoenix roots ran deep and long in comparison to her age. A mere eighteen years entangled her with the drug store clerk, the mayor, the pastor, the doctor, the blind man she taught to play accordion, neighbors, and even elementary school teachers of years gone by. She knew the city and the city knew her. Her name echoed off glass windows as she walked down the street. Invitations to entertain at notable events knew where to find her. The young girl envisioned cultivating the established roots of her life as her father had taught her during late-night irrigation sessions. However, a girl cannot be separated from her heart, and she contemplated giving her heart to the confident, handsome Air Force pilot.

Dances with Rabbit were archived in the movie reel of Virginia's mind when she landed an enviable summer job as an entertainer with Utah Parks Company's Grand Canyon Lodge at the North Rim. One of only two Arizonans offered a position; Virginia joined a group of highly talented entertainers that included students from the acclaimed Julliard Academy. Every evening the staff put on a talent show followed by a dance. Upper-class transcontinental travelers who arrived by tour bus and the occasional dignitary were guests at the lodge along with middle class families who took to the open roads in their automobiles. Each morning the staff lined up to sing a song to visitors as they left. The famous sing-away ceremony was a timeless lodge tradition.

Virginia fit in well with the festive atmosphere and soon became a favorite entertainer among the resort's visitors. The popular demand for her infectious stage presence spread far and wide. When special guests arrived at Zion National Park for the National Governors' Convention, she and her accordion were put on a bus to

Utah to perform for the prestigious crowd.

Her charisma was missed if she was off work for even a day. However, there was one event important enough for Virginia to request special permission to leave the lodge and take a bus back home -- Rabbit's graduation ceremony. Completing the advanced pilot training program was a major accomplishment; and the Air Force pulled out all the stops to congratulate the men for a job well done. High-ranking officers gave inspirational speeches, various aircraft were on display, the military band played festive music, and each pilot reveled in his own accomplishment.

The 51-Dog Class proved under Major Carter they could endure all types of punishment. They became the first jet class at Williams AFB to graduate without a fatality. Surviving Carter gave the Chain Gang more hope of surviving the North Koreans.

Virginia's parents, brother and sister, and the Hare family joined other families and friends of all of the men gathered at Williams AF Base for the grand occasion. Understanding that many of the honorees would soon ship out to fly in the Korean Conflict and may not return underlined the importance of the celebration.

The weight of that knowledge, the emotion of the day, and festive atmosphere all contributed to Virginia saying,

"Yes."

When Rabbit said, "Will you marry me?"

Immediately.

The giddy couple sneaked away from the graduation ceremony to their own impromptu wedding ceremony. June 25, 1951, with eyes sparkling with love and anticipation, the pair said, "I do," in front of an Air Force chaplain but the secret union was not revealed to a single soul.

Rabbit drove Virginia back to the North Rim and the lodge and then headed out to his new assignment at Nellis AFB in Las Vegas. His new post awarded leave much more freely than his unit at Williams received. Whenever he had a day or two off base, he drove five hours to the Grand Canyon to see Virginia. She introduced him to all of her friends, fellow entertainers, bar keepers, and chefs, but never as her husband. She would have lost her job and risked the news spreading to other parts of her life.

Summer ended, college at Arizona State began, and Rabbit went to war in Korea. The newlywed's secret remained safely hidden until Virginia's pregnancy became undeniable. Breaking the news to her parents meant breaking their hearts, but when she could delay no longer Virginia announced her marriage and pending arrival. Howard and Ruth were initially stunned, aghast, and struggled to organize thoughts and words together. They knew better than Virginia how much her life would change when she became a mother. With a little time to process the news and catch her breath, Ruth released her vision of Virginia as Miss Arizona. Putting her picture in the broken frame lost its importance. The soon-to-be grandparents embraced their daughter and her new reality wholeheartedly.

Soon news of Virginia's marriage and pending motherhood reached Mary Lou who couldn't hide her surprise or excitement for her Dami Phi friend who had formerly sworn off dating.

After high school graduation in 1951, Mary Lou found a state job working across the street from the Arizona Capital in the office of Financial Responsibilities. Employment here lasted about a year until friends from Tempe encouraged Mary Lou to enroll at Arizona State. Mary Lou and Virginia could become classmates once again. The elementary school principal and her farmer husband offered Mary Lou a place to live in return for helping them keep their house in order. With no real attachments to keep her in Phoenix, Mary Lou considered the offer a good one.

Since PUHS graduation, Mary Lou discarded one beau, Jim, and acquired another named Toby, each of whom had given her diamond engagement rings. "Two diamond rings" became her claim to fame. Mary Lou and Toby broke up before she went to Tempe to become a Sun Devil. In her unattached state, she quickly noticed Ira Fulton. Ira stuck in Virginia's memory from her previous summers marching through ASC band camp. He impressed her as a sport jock filled with unlimited cockiness. He could be heard announcing, to all who would listen, his ambition to be a millionaire by the age of thirty. What Virginia saw as arrogance, Mary Lou identified as charisma and drive. Soon Mary Lou had her third diamond ring and four months later they were married. Mary Lou supported Ira's goals as Mrs. Fulton; and he lived up to his proclamations of wealth, only a few years later than anticipated.

All of the girls, except Martha, had transitioned during the 50s from the frivolity of romance to the reality of marriage and babies. The chores and responsibilities they had seen their mothers take on were now theirs. They embraced the new roles with all of the excellence and determination previously applied to twirling, dancing, pompon, and school studies.

Marriage! What Have I Gotten Into?

Whatever vision and dreams of marriage the girls held, they looked nothing like the reality of unexpected illness, scraping by on pennies, and men leaving for war. The young wives dutifully followed their husbands into discomfort and uncertainty and sometimes endured extended time apart.

SNOOKIE AND GENE

After one year of college and football, Gene joined the Navy to fight in the Korean War. Boot camp in San Diego, California led to Frogman training in Corpus Christi, Texas. The precursor to the Navy SEALS, Frogman days were long and intense. Mornings came very early, consisted of miles of marching, hundreds of repetitions of exercises, and pushing the soldier's physical limits in extreme conditions.

Snookie considered the conditions extreme as well. The humidity of the gulf location gripped the now six-months pregnant wife in misery. She could not escape the invisible enemy of humidity as she and Gene searched for a place to live. They became boarders in several different rooms until finally finding a small apartment to match their tiny budget.

Relieved to have a place to prepare for the baby's arrival, Snookie relaxed long enough for Gene to announce they were moving again. He had located a rent-free apartment belonging to an elderly gentleman who required day-to-day living assistance in exchange. Two weeks later, Snookie delivered 9 lb. 13 oz. baby Jennifer.

Humidity proved to be too powerful a nemesis for the desert dwellers. Just weeks after Jennifer's arrival, Gene developed asthma and was discharged from the Navy. The young family scurried back to a dry climate.

SHIRLEY AND BOB

Bob's college football career was cut short in his second season when he contracted Valley Fever. The disease's only antidote is rest. The couple returned to Phoenix for Bob's recuperation and Shirley's delivery. She gave birth to a baby girl named Debbie the same month Jennie was born.

Bob regained his strength and enlisted in the Air Force as the Korean War intensified. Communications training had bonded Bob with his best friend, Delores. After training, the men were sent out according to their last name. Bob Cannon was assigned to Europe with the C's. The D's went to Korea where Delores was killed within weeks.

Bob's appreciation for the gift of life deepened his spiritual commitment. While in France, he and some buddies began gathering in tents to pray. They decided to try out a Sunday service on base, and the sermon was pretty good, so they attended again the following week. Curiosity filled the men when that sermon was identical to the first. They soon realized the chaplain preached only one sermon. Not long after, base authorities discovered the chaplain was an alcoholic drinking all of the wine intended for communion. With the chaplain discharged, Bob and his buddies decided to start their own Sunday service and began volunteering for different roles. The positions were quickly filled except for preaching and everyone agreed that would be Bob's task.

In a letter home, Bob let Shirley know he felt God calling him to become a minister, not a football coach as he'd planned. Shirley recognized Bob's speaking talent and believed he would make a great pastor, but she wasn't so sure she was cut out to be a pastor's wife.

BARBARA AND GENE

Upon college graduation, Gene accepted a teaching position at Stevenson Elementary in Phoenix while Barbara continued her studies. In 1954, she completed her degree in elementary education with an emphasis on kindergarten and primary education. Two years later she gave birth to their first child; Mark, and soon, the young family began a new life journey in El Paso, Texas.

VIRGINIA AND RABBIT

Virginia finished one semester of college and

then took correspondence courses while awaiting her spring arrival. Rabbit anxiously awaited the baby's birth as well and quickly devoured the letters that took six to eight weeks to reach Korea and often arrived in bunches. One spring day, Rabbit's friend, Red Dog, scooped up letters from mail call before flying a mission over highly-fortified Pongyang, North Korea. Wanting to have some fun at Rabbit's expense, he waited until they landed to unzip one of his flight suit pockets and hand Rabbit a letter.

He watched as Rabbit opened it, quickly read through, and asked, "Is there a baby yet?"

"No," Rabbit replied.

"Well, try this one," Red Dog said as he reached into a different pocket to extract another letter. "Is there a baby yet?"

"No," Rabbit replied.

"Why don't you read this one," Red Dog handed over a third letter. "Is there a baby yet?"

"No," Rabbit replied, unable to withhold his frustration.

"Maybe this one," Red Dog grinned as he held out yet another letter that Rabbit snatched from his grip.

"Still no baby," Rabbit reported.

"Well how about this," as Red Dog's eyes danced with immense self satisfaction and shared joy as he reached into his breast pocket and pulled out a cablegram announcing the birth of eight pound, eight-and-a-half ounce Audrey Denise Hare. The strong desire to punch Red Dog that had been steadily growing inside Rabbit over the previous ten minutes melted into bear hugs and congratulations.

Mother and daughter settled into a routine until Daddy came home to meet his new family in May. Their darling baby girl soon took on the name Bunni in keeping with Hare tradition and was christened at Phoenix's First United Methodist Church.

Rabbit thought Virginia's new joy of motherhood would overshadow her desire for a college degree. He was wrong. His one hundred twelve Korean combat mission finished, Rabbit whisked the young family off to Bryan, Texas and his next duty station. He began training more pilots for the Korean conflict and rented a furnished duplex behind Texas A & M College. The small family began lasting friendships with neighbors on all sides, including professors who shared vegetables from their gardens. The all-boys school offered coed classes in the summer, and Virginia was first to enroll. On her way to claiming another twelve credit hours, Virginia's doctor placed her on bed rest to avoid miscarrying in her second pregnancy. With finals just weeks away, her education psychology professor declared she had earned an A by maintaining the highest grade in the class throughout the term. Her English professor assigned an incomplete to her transcript until she could take her final exam, which she did six weeks later. A healthy little brother, Allan joined toddler Bunni for the Hare's move from the wide expanse of Texas to the desert of Arizona and on to the southern drawl of South Carolina.

MARY LOU AND IRA

Ira was the youngest of eleven children in a family of the Mormon faith. Mary Lou gladly took the necessary steps to become a member of the faith so she and Ira could marry in the temple. After the wedding, Ira set out to accomplish his goal to amass wealth. He worked hard, sometimes holding down two or three jobs at once. Building his fortune took a few years longer than he predicted, but along the way he generously helped his family and always managed to get his Mary Lou what she wanted.

MARTHA

After completing her education degree at the University of Arizona, Martha taught P.E. in the San Diego school system long enough to discover it was the wrong career path for her. She found another job with the Frazee Paint Company. It turned out to be a place where she could grow and thrive.

As all of the girls of Dami Phi Datum began to experience life through marriage, motherhood, illness, wars, tight budgets, and new jobs in new cities, they realized there might have been a time when they could do without boys, but there was never a time they could do without each other.

The Dope

High school graduations scattered the Dami Phi girls in all directions. Early club members, Joyce Berutti and Zelpha Ellenbaum, drifted away and had limited contact with the other girls. Whatever her current address, they each had families to come home to in Phoenix. When some were in town at the same time, they got together, sometimes with husbands, always with children, to catch up and relive old times. These gatherings were infrequent and only included a few of the girls at a time.

Shirley learned of some friends who stayed connected by circulating what was known as a Round Robin letter. When a person received the package of letters, she removed the letter she had written and replaced it with a new one. Then the package was sent to the next person who did the same. Everyone loved the idea!

The Round Robin began with Shirley writing from Moses Lake AFB, Washington a letter containing all the current news of her life and mailing it to Snookie in Wilcox, Arizona who read Shirley's letter and wrote one of her own. Snookie sent both letters on to Martha in San Diego. Martha added a letter and sent the three to Mary Lou in Tempe. Mary Lou contributed to both the news and the bulk of the package that went into a new envelope addressed to Virginia.

Keeping up with Virginia's address was a challenge Mary Lou tackled. As the letters started in 1955, Virginia and Rabbit were enroute pipeline to Sembach, Germany via Luke AFB, Arizona and Shaw AFB, South Carolina. Waiting for all of their paperwork and passports to clear, they spent months zig-zagging across the country in their blue and white station wagon.

Virginia truly thrived on staying in contact with friends and poured her thoughts over paper covering it from edge to edge, top to bottom, and front to back. She then sent the package on to Barbara in El Paso, who enjoyed reading far more than writing. The letters waited weeks and sometimes months for Barbara to set aside her dread of writing, put pen to paper, and complete the circle back to Shirley in Washington. Shirley removed her letter, replaced it with a new one, then sent them all to Snookie, and around the letters went.

The Dami Phi friends quickly became addicted to receiving the news the letters brought, getting responses to their questions, and learning from the tips shared about household and family management, school, community involvement, and fashion. Envelopes grew to accommodate photos of children, news clippings about classmates, and other brochures or invitations of interest. Packages arrived with great anticipation and excitement. So much so, it became known as The Dope.

Addiction to The Dope sustained their friendship and wove the young women more tightly together. The fix Virginia received from the news of home became even more important as the Air Force found need of Rabbit in Europe. Within a year of beginning the Round Robin letters, Virginia's pilot received orders to move her, Bunni, Allan, and now infant Rhonda along for the journey to Germany. The family of five launched a weeks-long road trip for their U.S. farewell tour.

This third pregnancy proved more difficult for Virginia due to increased risk from a negative Rh factor and severe arthritis taking up residence in her hip joints. Rabbit's leave from the Air Force while the family waited for passports to arrive couldn't have come at a better time. Virginia relied heavily upon his help. They spent weeks traveling through Texas, Oklahoma, and on to New York visiting family and friends along the way to introduce Rhonda and say, "So long for now."

Family and friends saw first-hand the toll three pregnancies had taken on Virginia. Not even her brightest smile could hide the fact she could not stand without assistance. The vicious attack of arthritis caused considerable discomfort but deep gratitude for Rabbit's timely leave. Her doctors insisted Rhonda must be the youngest member of the Hare family. Another pregnancy would only exacerbate the problem.

Even immobility could not stop tireless Virginia as they traversed the countryside in their car filled with luggage, children, and the family's beloved Dachshund Skoshe, who traveled with four new pups of her own. As the pedigreed puppies grew to weaning age, they were given to family and friends stretching from the east coast to Arizona.

Perhaps bolstered by the popularity of her lineage or maybe unaware of canine traditions in the deep woods of NE Oklahoma, Skoshe grew over confident during one visit. She got too close to Friday, a large coon hound during feeding time. The poor little momma left the altercation with her scalp laid open. Skoshe endured the one hundred mile trip to the nearest veterinarian and received a number of stitches. The doc expressed concern over Skoshe's schedule to be shipped to Germany the next week. She needed more time to heal before such a journey.

Not even a sick dog can deter the military's schedule, and the Hare's reported to port call at Fort Hamilton, New York. However, the one-week stay in New York became more than two when Russia sent tanks and troops into Budapest to reassert communist rule over protestors.

Within ten days Russian military killed 30,000 Hungarian demonstrators and reclaimed authority and order by instilling unquestionable fear into the hearts of all citizens. The Hares were now cleared to travel into Germany and Skoshe had regained enough strength and healing for her long trip.

Stationed in Sembach, Germany; Virginia delighted as the Round Robin letters came. Ink splashed upon paper in a meaningful pattern celebrated milestones, offered condolences, and gave heed to the trivial.

Babies were born. A miscarriage suffered. Church attended. Crawling. A first tooth. Walking. Haircuts and new glasses. Dinners prepared. Committees formed. Classes taken. Curtains and costumes sewn. The Dami Phi friends shared life through letters.

Letters were the only affordable means of communication. Long distance telephone calls were expensive, and international calls were reserved for high-ranking officials and business deals with many zeros. A first-class stamp cost four cents (1960), and the airmail rate jumped to seven cents per ounce. Mary Lou had the most disposable income to apply toward the international postage so keeping up with Virginia's address became her responsibility. Virginia did her best to keep Mary Lou updated as to her whereabouts in spite of the unpredictable nature of the military.

Package in hand, anticipation greeted every personal note. Eyes lingered over words, the sound, the meaning, the thickness of the letters, and slant of script. The folded paper was a connection to family, home, friends, and life, which became even more precious during overseas assignments.

While home and news from home became Virginia's anchor, she had to embrace her surroundings and live in the present. That meant developing meaningful and caring relationships with those surrounding her.

Germany

It was 1956, the occupation had ended, and West Germany's capitalistic economy was booming. Restitution for war had been paid, and the allies realized German manufacturing was needed for all of Europe's economy. Virtually every German had a job, including the thousands of defectors who left the Russian controlled East for the democracy of the West before the massive Berlin wall was constructed to keep its citizens in. Germany proceeded to recruit more than one million workers from neighboring countries to fill the job demand.

At Sembach Air Base, it seemed half of the cars were Volkswagens, a true rarity in the U.S. At seventeen cents per gallon, Virginia could drive all week for a dollar. The small car was plenty big enough for Rabbit, the three small children, and herself.

Traffic in the air lacked the efficiency of the cute automobiles. Rabbit did not approve of the local air-traffic habits, and his concerns had reached the ears of Colonel Franklin Nichols. After six planes and several pilots were lost in three mid-air collisions, Colonel Nichols assigned Rabbit the new role of Flying Safety Officer. His exact orders were to "fix it."

Suddenly Rabbit was in charge of all aspects of wing air safety: procedures, pilot training, air-traffic control, and accident investigation. The need for better safety practices was great, and Rabbit dedicated himself to the task. He dropped everything to personally travel to accident sites, investigate the cause, and implement measures for preventions. The unpredictable nature of plane crashes and Rabbit's immediate response prompted Virginia to coin the phrase, "Rabbit is always coming home." She chose to anticipate the positive rather than dread the negative. He often received emergency calls requiring him to leave immediately for a crash site. Downed planes beckoned him in the wee hours of morning, on holidays, and without notice to airfields scattered across Europe, mountains unfriendly toward metal birds, over seas, and other continents.

Virginia became a skilled juggler. She expertly tossed into the air Rabbit's erratic travel schedule, surprise dinner guests, school for Bunni and her own college courses, volunteer roles in the officer's wives club, sewing clothes, caring for their children and maintained it all with an outward grace and poise that required large doses of struggle and grit. She never counted on Rabbit's assistance but always felt grateful when he was there. His presence added a certain unpredictability to the mix that was sure to add interest and drama to her letters.

Virginia corresponded with many other friends and family outside of the Dami Phi Datum Round Robin. Virginia's and Rabbit's parents watched their grandchildren grow up in the home movies Virginia mailed. The tapes traveled somewhat like the Round Robin letters. The Howell's received the movies, shared them with nearby friends, then forwarded them on to the Hare's. After the movies were viewed by all interested parties in the U.S., they traveled back to Germany for safe-keeping.

In an effort to experience more of Europe,

Virginia took the children to the island of Mallorca in the Mediterranean for a vacation. For two months they swam, played on the beach, soaked up the sun, and did absolutely no cooking or cleaning. Rabbit joined them for another two weeks of relaxation. The peace of mind generated by the much-needed time away from the demands of the Air Force was interrupted by Virginia's suspicions of a fourth pregnancy. Her doctor was firm in his order of no more children. Virginia's hip joints barely survived the third pregnancy and her negative Rh blood factor increased the potential complications for both her and the baby. Her doctor was very concerned.

Rabbit and Virginia agreed they would tell no one at home about this pregnancy. The well-meaning words of advice from friends and the deep concern and worry of parents would do nothing to change the situation. Luckily, Virginia's doctor was their neighbor, and his frequent house calls relieved the couple's minds – as well as the doctor's.

Within a short amount of time, she once again could not walk unassisted. Five-year-old

Bunni carried baby Rhonda around and helped prepare her bottles while Virginia crawled into the living room of their small apartment each morning to emcee the circus of play, reading, singing, and naps.

When conducting life from the floor no longer worked, Virginia was hospitalized for three months in the big USAF hospital in Weisbaden. Cortisone shots, heat treatments, and physical therapy worked to loosen her joints while generous neighbors cared for the children. Rabbit followed the doctor's orders to move the family to a first floor apartment. Virginia was no longer allowed to climb stairs and certainly forbidden (again) to have any more babies!

Through the letters, the girlfriends compared pregnancies, but Virginia kept hers a secret. She didn't want her friends to worry when there was absolutely nothing they could do to help her. She especially didn't want her parents to worry, so she kept the anticipation of their fourth child within their circle of friends in Germany.

The Dami Phi ladies were unaware of the irony when Virginia shared the Hare's New

Year's resolutions in a letter written February 1958, only two-and-a-half months before the expected arrival.

The Hare's rang in the New Year of 1958 with resolve:

1. No more pregnancies!
2. Relax and enjoy life.
3. Take advantage of European travel.
4. Be more patient with the kids.

Virginia finally shared the news of their pending arrival in April's letter. She retold the story of her stubborn joints, months in the hospital, and the extra special, VIP treatment received from her doctor, Bill Rowlett, who was also their neighbor. The convenience of house calls eventually was replaced by a forty-minute drive to Army hospital, Second General in Landstuhl, once each week. The doctor's caution regarding potential complications due to Virginia's Rh factor prompted early induction. Three and a half weeks prior to the due date, Virginia spent two days in the hospital sipping castor oil cocktails and trotting to the bathroom. That didn't work, so plan B took her to the delivery room where the membrane was stripped followed by five hours of mild labor. Finally an x-ray revealed a closed cervix and Virginia was sent home where she received The Dope and wrote letters while waiting to go into labor.

Rabbit waited too. The Air Force allowed him to postpone a trip to North Africa, but he hurried off to investigate a crash at Phalsbourg, France. The accident took the lives of that base commander and a captain, leaving two wives and nine children behind.

While Rabbit dealt with the tragedy of death, Virginia celebrated the new life of baby Valerie, born May 1, 1958. This time she gave natural childbirth a try along with the new fad of "rooming in" with the baby. When Rabbit returned, the sight of a healthy mom and tightly wrapped blanket topped with a carpet of brown curls filled him with joy. Adored by her siblings, Valerie easily claimed her spot in the Hare family despite the fact Allan called her "my baby brother" for weeks.

Virginia's recovery continued, and five months later she was able to climb stairs and even chase after the children. Her daily schedule included trips to the base hospital for heat treatments to loosen her joints and relieve some of the pain. By summertime she was enjoying the long summer days with sunrise at 4:00 a.m. and sunset after 8:00 p.m.

The Round Robin letters became a diary of Virginia's life. She wrote about following through with their New Year's resolution to see more of Europe. She and Rabbit traveled to the Austrian Alps for snow skiing with glorious views followed by warm drinks by a cozy lodge fire. They visited the bunker of Hitler and Eva Braun, traversing the stark 180-foot descent they found riddled with bullet holes. A drive to Laon, France took them past areas that had seen heavy fighting in World War II. Along the road were trenches, gun fortifications, underground hangers, airstrips, and many, many graves.

The extended light of day made it impossible to hide the fifteen-year-old scars of war. Trenches lazily rested beside roadways and crumbled pieces of buildings anchored memories, lest they blow away with the breeze. The emptiness of the underground hangers and gun fortifications echoed throughout the large cemeteries filled with simple stone markers. The landmarks reminded them of the tyranny of the Fuehrer. The same scars on the other side of the Berlin Wall aroused memories of American bombs determined to ruin the "perfect society" touted by East German propaganda.

The letters chronicled the weather; constant muddy grounds of spring, long hours of daylight in summer, the beauty of fall, and snowy adventures of winter. Each season brought about new family activities as well as different laundry and housekeeping requirements.

Part of Virginia's prescription was hiring a maid. Inger washed her windows every other day and buffed the linoleum floors daily. When the topic of house cleaning arose in the letters, the friends shared efficient ways to regularly wash the walls and baseboards, launder and iron the drapes. The key to keeping a tidy home was a strict weekly schedule. Virginia recommended good help as the best cleaning tip of all. Once everything was sparkly clean, the Air Force had a way of shaking things up.

France

"Our wing is moving to France," said Rabbit one night over dinner.

"When," Virginia asked?

"Fairly soon", he replied and explained they would be one of the first families to move since they were approaching the one year in-theater deadline.

News of the move didn't faze Virginia much except for the fact they had only been allowed to bring clothes and personal items to Germany. Their quarters were furnished complete with silver service and china. Sending for the stored household items in Texas meant they would arrive near the end of the one-year duration in France.

The couple decided to invest in modern teakwood Danish Furniture. Europeans raved over its style and durability. Rabbit and Virginia drove to the Army Officers Club in Heidelburg to examine the traveling Scandinavian-style furniture display currently making the rounds of military bases. They selected a sofa, an occasional chair, and a coffee table for the living room, plus a dining table with six chairs and a buffet. The bedrooms would be filled with stacking teakwood chests, a set of beechwood Danish bunk beds for the two older children with the current baby crib and playpen sufficing for the two little ones to sleep in. Careful not to order too much, they knew the quarters in France were to be considerably smaller than the current unit in Sembach.

Inger, the family's wonderful Danish maid, agreed to help through the move. She packed boxes, wrangled children, and assisted in all that needed to be done. Arriving in France, the Hare's were greeted with exposed water pipes running along the baseboards of their three bedroom duplex. The pipes leaked horrifically contributing to abundant mold. Virginia insisted on painting all of the walls before moving in. She and Rabbit worked fast using rollers with flat water based paint, which dried fairly quickly. As soon as the Hare's settled in France, Inger returned to Germany and her fiancé. Virginia was left to manage the duplex some fourteen miles from Laon Air Base, and no telephone was nearby.

The fuel oil tank for the furnace dominated the kitchen, another unwelcome feature. Even the furnace gave center stage to the old Kenmore washing machine that sat right in front of the kitchen sink for drainage. Running off a transformer, the Kenmore washed only half-size loads and was quite inefficient. This left hardly any room for food preparation, so the washer top doubled as an island prep center.

Soon Rabbit expanded his photography interest, and the kitchen began to serve as a dark room as well. The work surface of the washer was most useful in helping develop photos in the dark of night. Already doing the triple duty of kitchen, laundry, and dark room, it was the only room in the house that didn't have a clothesline. The damp, dark weather of northeast France supplied enough humidity to require two to three days for a diaper to dry. Two little ones in diapers resulted in clothes hanging from lines throughout the house continuously.

After a few months of wet clothes flapping

him in the face, Rabbit ordered a clothes dryer through the Base Exchange. The new appliance joined the oil tank and the washing machine in the already crowded kitchen and tripled the electric bill. The master of the house was happy with the absence of clotheslines and flapping diapers as he floated in and out between his temporary duties with the squadron and plane crash investigations throughout Europe. Virginia was left with figuring out how to cook in a kitchen equipped with wall-to-wall appliances.

Virginia's letter to her friends revealed her plague of grey hair and a few extra pounds gained during her pregnancies. Never willing to complain, she preceded her lament with the fact she was well enough to lead an active life and that meant the world. Her arthritis had greatly improved and she hardly sat still for a moment.

On arrival at Laon AFB, one of the first people Virginia met was the Wing Chaplain. She had two babies not yet christened and wanted to schedule two baptisms. Chaplain Dickinson refused. As a hard-core Baptist, he only performed immersion baptism. Virginia would not be easily deterred.

"In baptizing my children, I see it as a commitment to bring them up in a Christian home with Christian beliefs but with respect for others wherever we might be stationed," said Virginia.

Chaplain Dickinson listened to her request and accepted the challenge of finding a solution. He located a French Huguenot willing to baptize the children. By the time he was able to finalize Virginia's request, nineteen more children were signed up for the christening ceremony.

The all-important Sunday morning arrived in March of 1959. The religious rites of baptism were scheduled in Chapel No.1 at 1030 hours. The family readied themselves for the big day. Hat, gloves, hose, and high heels for Virginia, the absolute Sunday best for the children, and a flight suit for Rabbit. While preparing for church, he was called to investigate a fighter plane crash in another country. He grabbed his B-4 bag and jet helmet, helped get the kids in the car, and Virginia dropped Rabbit off at the flight line on her way to the chapel.

Situating Bunni and Allan in a pew with her

good friend Faye O'Grady, Virginia took nine-month-old baby Valerie in her arms and held tightly the hand of lively, energetic, not-yet-two-year-old Rhonda. Virginia and her two little ones joined the line of parents and children at the altar.

The beautiful ceremony began with Reverend Etinne Lacombe presiding and the base translator repeating in English. Each christening was performed with the Huguenot and translator standing side by side. Little Valerie seemed disinterested in both languages and amused herself by grabbing for Virginia's hat. Virginia instinctively released Rhonda's hand as she reached for the toppling adornment. As if Rhonda had been waiting for that exact moment, the bundle of lace and frills shot down the center aisle intent on the front door. Everyone participating in the ceremony froze as Faye O'Grady quickly jumped up and grabbed the racing Rhonda. Faye carried the wriggling toddler to the altar amid ripples of light laughter.

Filled with compassion, Chaplain Dickinson stepped down from the altar to take Valerie from

Virginia's arms whispering, "I think you need a little help, Virginia."

The ceremony continued with Valerie in Chaplain Dickinson's arms and Virginia holding Rhonda. Virginia was touched by Chaplain Dickinson's aid and support of his military family during a ceremony at odds with his own beliefs. He stood by her and the oath he took to become a military chaplain. Always remembering his kindness and helpfulness in her time of need, Virginia maintained correspondence with Chaplain Dickinson and his family for many years.

Amidst the gloom of the war-torn countryside, Faye's husband Joe O'Grady decided entertainment was in order. The 302nd Squadron would do a show at the Officers Club. A skilled manager, Joe began assigning roles and responsibilities. No rated members of the squadron, including the wives, were spared. Virginia offered her support immediately and fell right into the familiar role of entertainer.

The format of the show was based on the popular Ed Sullivan Show. Polly Pedjoe was dubbed the scriptwriter. Army Liaison Officer, Major Scott, with a background in vaudeville, became Ned Sledivan. A singing chorus was formed with Faye assigned as director. Virginia became a part of a harem of dancing girls plus was assigned an accordion act while Rabbit took on the role of backstage hand.

In true show must go on spirit, Virginia and the other harem dancers, Caryl Tarrant, Sylvia Frank, Barbara Kartun, and Eileen Walen sacrificed their grocery money to purchase costume fabric. The ladies sewed filmy, pink chiffon with a lining of pink cotton into two-piece, bare-midriff outfits trimmed with black braid. They begged and borrowed an assortment of rhinestone necklaces to drape across their foreheads and all kinds of bangles to adorn arms and ankles. Practices were filled with so much fun and laughter; no one seemed concerned that their cupboards grew bare.

Three days until payday, Caryl burst through the door of Virginia's duplex waving a fistful of paper money and yelling at the top of her lungs, "We eat tonight! Virginia, we can eat tonight!"

She threw a five dollar bill and two ones at her shocked friend as she then raced out the back kitchen door, across the yard, and on up toward her quarters on the hill behind. Somehow, from someone, Caryl had found a source to help reimburse the mighty sum of seven dollars each!

The night of the show finally arrived. Performers and audience lined up for a chicken buffet dinner and a night full of laughs. The Officer's Club hadn't seen such a crowd in ages. Major Scott led the way as the emcee, with Joe O'Grady, dressed in a dapper suit as the back up announcer and director. The singing chorus performed in red turtleneck tops with black skirts or trousers.

Virginia took the stage with her accordion in an outfit made in Palma de Majorca. The black top sat above a hand-woven wool skirt. Big false eyelashes, black dangling earrings, and tall spiked high heels added stage-worthy pizzazz. She played the toe tapping, lively Los Rancheros while a tall, debonair 1st Lieutenant new to the squadron, performed a flamenco dance. To the delight of the audience, he had to drop out of the act when the heel of his shoe broke. Virginia continued playing accompanied by roars of laughter and applause from the crowd.

The advertisements between acts were truly the hits of the show. A Volkswagen convertible driven into the Officers Club featured Ernie and Joyce Meis in the back seat. It was dubbed "the biggest little bug in the small car field." Another was John Zartman, a normally somber West Point graduate, dressed only in combat boots, a jet helmet and a diaper. He was introduced as Johnet Pilgrim, the playmate the playgirls would most like to smoke off with.

Doc Kartun, the newest flight surgeon, played the role of Old Dope Peddler, singing and throwing little white boxes filled with APC's to the crowd. His wife Barbara did her own interpretation of a striptease. She sang Zip Goes Your Zipper pretending to emerge from the flying suit she was wearing while flipping the many zippers. An old fashioned melodrama complete with a nasty villain in a flowing black cape delighted the audience. Thespians emoted under flickering lights. The crowd doubled over in laughter.

The show captured the headline of the base newspaper: THE 302nd "TV PARTY".....SMASH HIT! The show was such a success that they took it on the road and played at the Noncommissioned Officers Club the following week.

Virginia's glamorous tales of travel through Europe and base stage productions contrasted with the Cold War reality. She welcomed the announcement of new orders – a return state-side even if it was to . . . Wisconsin.

Home Again, Sort Of

The Hare family rolled into the capital city of Madison as the Wisconsin Badger football team embarked on a Big Ten Championship year, 1959. Rabbit joined Flying Safety Officers at Air Defense Headquarters at Truax Field. America's dairyland couldn't hold them for long. The Hares had bought a house, unpacked their boxes, enrolled in school, and then eagerly headed southwest to visit family and friends. Rabbit received leave for Christmas followed by orders to an intensive two-month flying safety course at the University of Southern California.

That solo assignment meant two glorious months for Virginia and the children to remain under the sunny skies of Phoenix instead of the frigid Wisconsin winter. It was Christmas, Mickey, home from college, and Patricia, still in high school, couldn't get enough of their nieces and nephew. It was their first time to meet Valerie, who was twenty months old, and marvel at how all of the children had grown and changed. The children loved playing among the trees Virginia had helped her father plant and enjoyed the pecans that she once thought would never mature. Bunni and Allan harvested figs and plums with Rhonda keeping up as best she could.

It seemed everyone was in town for Christmas. Virginia's faithful Dami Phi friends planned a reunion. All six met at Encanto Park in Phoenix on a beautiful December day. Young mothers with children and picnic lunches in tow quickly became giggling high school girls all over again. The large park had a playground, duck pond, and a lake with fishing and boating. They experienced it all and had a great time. Neither dwelling in the past nor dreaming of the future, they lived in the moment and enjoyed each other in the here and now. No one passed judgment or attempted to fulfill a false image; only understanding existed between the fast friends. Each one spent the day forgetting who they were expected to be and relaxed into being herself.

The setting sun reminded the true friends they would inevitably disperse. Their light and easy goodbyes came from knowing their friendship would easily continue through the constant circle of letters.

Virginia receives her long-awaited diploma from Dr. Collier, Northeast Oklahoma University president, May 1980.

Virginia's graduation picture finally made it into the broken frame, May of 1980 after completing her studies at Northeastern State University, Tahlequah, Oklahoma.

Jeff Taylor, one of Virginia's outstanding students, carries the Olympic torch across Tulsa, 1984.

Gathering at the University of Oklahoma, Virginia inspires 416 delegates at Oklahoma Girls State 2007, while doing her patriotic leadership thing. Virginia served as president of the American Legion Auxiliary Department of Oklahoma 2006-07. ALA has sponsored Oklahoma Girls State since 1940.

Virginia teams up with other Oklahomans to lobby on Capital Hill for Veterans Affairs. Left to right: BJ Longenbaugh [Noble], Virginia Hare [Grove], Senator Jim Inhofe, Sue Heil [Stillwater]. Through the years Virginia helped push for TRICARE support as promised by Congress. As promises were broken Virginia persevered and supported POW Bud Day who took the case all the way to the Supreme Court along with the flag amendment, and many other issues concerning veterans and survivors.

Once all of the children were grown and Ira and Mary Lou accumulated more wealth, the Dami Phi's reunions became weeklong affairs hosted in one of the Fulton's homes. This is the first extended gathering at Mary Lou's lodge in Pinetop, Arizona in 1981. Left to right front; Mary Lou, Martha, and Virginia, back; Snookie, Shirley, and Barbara.

Celebrating Independence Day at the Coronado Dami Phi reunion of 1995. The Coronado Island celebration outdid all others the ladies had ever seen.

USS Kitty Hawk rolled out the red carpet for the Dami Phi's at Virginia's request, thanks to Captain Dennis Deakins. The impressive tour started as Captain Deakins led the ladies through saluting ensigns as he was piped onto the ship. Left to right; Virginia, Dennis, ship's doctor, Shirley, Mary Lou, and ship's corpsman.

Have bags, will travel. The Dami Phi friends were never accused of traveling light. Barbara even packed a frozen Mexican casserole in layers of dry ice and Styrofoam. Virginia, Shirley, Barbara, and Snookie await Mary Lou's pick up in San Diego for the start of an anticipated reunion.

The 2005, 4th of July Dami Phi reunion celebration at the Stadium of Fire, Provo, Utah. The girls were treated like royalty and greeted by Debbie Reynolds before her concert performance. Barbara, Shirley, Virginia, Debbie Reynolds, Snookie, and Mary Lou with Art, their trusted escort looking on.

Virginia and Ira share laughs at the Fulton Christmas open house in Auwatukee, Arizona in 2008. Ira and Mary Lou were known for their annual Christmas celebration the first Monday of December.

Mary Lou's 80th birthday celebration is well attended by Dami Phi friends. Snookie, Virginia, and Shirley join the party hosted by ASU president Dr. Michael Crow and his wife at the ASU Fulton Center, Tempe, Arizona 2013.

Sarah, Bunni, Patricia, and Virginia made the most of a longtime dream of a three day Mardi Gras adventure in New Orleans, Baton Rouge, Ville d' Platte, Louisiana.

Virginia, Class of 1951, brother Mickey, Class of 1957, and sister Patricia, Class of 1963 enjoyed the PUHS [Phoenix Union High School] Alumni Picnic, March 2014. Hundreds of classmates came together to recall memories and reconnect relationships. Patricia, twirling, and Virginia, playing her accordion, reclaimed their usual spotlight as featured entertainment for the crowd.

Toasting "1302" by Taos, New Mexico artist John Farnsworth -- his rendition of the adobe house at 1302 South 31st Avenue where the three grew up. Farnsworth captured Ruth's prolific rose garden and the now mature trees Harold and Virginia planted together years ago. Patricia, Mickey, and Virginia.

Virginia continues to attend Air Force reunions, flying solo since Rabbit's death. A highlight from the 2012 Voodoo Reconnaissance Pilot's reunion was a tour of Seattle's Dale Chihuly exhibit with the added pleasure of meeting the artist himself. Here they pose with Chihuly inspired umbrellas much needed in the downpour. Bob and Marj Gould, Kathrine Higgins, Mary Goldfein, Gretchen Harvell, and Virginia.

Teen flying and airplane partners Audrey "Rabbit" and Merlin, shared a lifelong passion for flying and all aircraft. Here at the Bartlesville Antique Bi-wing Air Show, May 1991. Left to right: Another pilot, Verne Griffin, Dr. Darrell Veit, Rabbit, Virginia, and Merlin pose with a Stearman owned by Dr. Veit, from Wisconsin. Allan covered the event for the Tulsa World.

Virginia treasures her many connections with vintage friends. These PUHS friends share stories over breakfast when Virginia comes to the Valley of the Sun. Charlie Kishiyama, retired Tempe police officer, Snookie, Virginia, and Windy McDonald, retired race car announcer and author.

Snookie and Virginia delight in the spectacular mountain views from the Tucson home of artist Diana Madaras. The Dami Phi pair are filled with excitement to be in the home of their favorite artist and enjoy the glorious evening with Diana in her studio gallery setting. Born and raised in Arizona, the two friends never tire of remarkable desert presentations of visual beauty in all art forms.

There's always something to do with Papa Rabbit from checking cows to catching crappie. Here he is on an excursion assisted by grandchildren Aaron, Sarah, Emily, Ashley, and Andrew.

The fish are biting! Terry Palmore, one of the Hares Hawaii SCUBA instructors, and his wife Kay reeled them in on their Grand Lake fishing excursion near Rabbit and Virginia's home. The Palmores also retired to NE Oklahoma after Terry's tour of duty as USAF recruiter in Tulsa.

Aussie Mac Cottrell greeted Rabbit with his first in-country FAC checkout in Lai Khe, Vietnam. The two flew with the Big Red One commanded by General Patton's son. Mac and his wife, Fran, enjoyed a visit with the Hares and experiencing rural Oklahoma life, October 2000.

Virginia's family celebrated her 80th birthday Vegas style ziplining down Fremont Street, enjoying shows, and lunch at Virginia's favorite restaurant. Virginia with Rhonda and granddaughters Emily and Gregorye.

Virginia's request for "No 80th Birthday Celebration," worked out differently than she expected. A storming of Las Vegas by family and friends from Arizona, Oklahoma, and California became a milestone to remember. Virginia's "Around the World' traveling buddy, Jennie Horn from San Francisco, provided the headquarters and hub of activity. They ate food, watched shows, tested their luck, and all even did the ZIPLINE.

A Graduation Picture for the Broken Frame

The women of Dami Phi Datum grew up observing their mothers work fulltime at housekeeping. Cooking, cleaning, and sewing were labor intensive and very time consuming. It was a time when only single women were allowed to teach alongside men in many schools. After many of the men left to fight in World War II, a few women that the girls knew went to work in factories, and for the first time, they witnessed married women filling empty classrooms in Phoenix Secondary Schools.

The Dami Phi girls became wives in the 1950s, mothers to teens in the 1960s, and empty nesters in the 1970s. Modern appliances and convenient food items meant housekeeping was no longer a fulltime job. Women in the workplace had won laws supporting equal pay and condemning sexual harassment. The workplace changed to better accommodate women and some of the Dami Phi friends never lost career mindsets from high school dreams.

Barbara pursued her career right out of high school. She became a reading specialist and taught first grade for twenty-eight years in El Paso, Texas. The hours and vacation schedule allowed her to be available anytime her two children, Mark and Linda, needed her. Martha never had children and advanced in her position at S. R. Frazee Company. The Frazee family bought out a couple of competitors, expanded the business, and moved Martha into a supervisory position at the Phoenix warehouse. She managed the accounts of the many paint contractors in the Valley of the Sun.

By the time Mary Lou's children were grown, she had expanded her volunteer activities and became more involved in philanthropy. She and Ira worked hard, accumulated wealth, and gave it away. Mary Lou's unplanned career allowed her to become a benevolent contributor of both time and money to their church, education, medical research, and individuals in need. Shirley raised six children with Bob. Although she was quite busy with family, the yearning to make a difference outside her own home persisted. She found great fulfillment in giving swim lessons to babies and small children. After her own children were grown, she also worked several years at the University of Arizona's scientific research facility, Biosphere 2.

Virginia and Snookie fully committed to responsibilities of wife and mother while holding onto dreams of a career someday. When their children graduated college, Virginia and Snookie eagerly sought out the education and training they desired. The aspiration for a job was something neither husband understood or supported. The men had worked for years and were looking forward to retirement. Even Martha had chosen to retire before Frazee sold out to German owners. However, Virginia and Snookie were just loosening up, eager to start a career.

In 1978, Snookie's two children were out of the nest. She enrolled at Lamson's Business College for refresher courses and short hand instruction. Her interest in politics motivated her to try for legislative secretary in the Arizona House of Representatives. Snookie applied, interviewed, and landed the job. Placed with newly elected representative, Carl Kunsek -- a pharmacy owner in Mesa, Snookie learned the ways of the legislature and loved every moment. Her amazement at how two floors of politicians, democrat and republican, and their staffs worked together in cooperation never ceased. After two terms, Representative Kunsek was appointed chairman of the Health Committee and Snookie's field of influence expanded as well. When Carl moved to the Arizona Senate and eventually became president of the Senate, Snookie was there to manage his office and observe the Meechum impeachment proceedings.

Valerie, Virginia's youngest, proudly wore her mortarboard hat and walked across the stage to receive her degree from Oklahoma State University in 1980. Ruth gently lifted the frame with the cracked glass off the wall in her Phoenix home. Time had darkened the plaster around the rectangular shape. The all-important frame possessed a sense of belonging even when it was removed. Valerie's graduation photo replaced Rhonda's and the newly dusted legacy hung proudly.

Valerie graduated with a major in vocational home economics and a minor in science. She also soloed her first flight toward a pilot's license. Rabbit saw to it that each of his children knew how to fly an airplane. Flight instruction took place below their house on the grass runway he cleared himself as well as at the Grove Airport that he managed for nine years.

Virginia celebrated Valerie's accomplishments as well as her own education adventure. She met with an advisor at Northeastern State University who helped determine she needed fifty-eight hours of course work, plus a semester of student teaching to obtain an education degree. Virginia's desire to complete the fifty-eight hours in only one year was met with concern from her advisor. Virginia convinced the advisor she could not be deterred, and she was sent to visit with the academic dean to get permission to carry such an unusually heavy workload.

Virginia's profound desire and strong determination could not be denied. She was granted permission, cloaked with both caution and encouragement. Virginia dove into her work and gave each course her very best effort. She received unlimited support from her professors.

Philanthropy had been instilled since childhood, and Virginia cared deeply about her volunteer work in the community. She chose to maintain her regular schedule of activities during the intense school year. Always able to run full speed on only four hours of sleep, she cut back to three. She put enormous pressure on herself and somehow kept it all together. Rabbit may have been the only other one who suffered her grueling schedule. He rarely saw her that year.

Virginia excelled in all classes and developed relationships with her professors. She proved just as passionate about learning as she felt about teaching. A couple of months away from completing her fifty-eight hours of course work, she looked forward to student teaching the next semester – her final semester.

It was then that, Virginia received news that her mother was ill and didn't have much longer to live. She began looking for a small break in her studies to work in an Arizona visit. It was foremost on her mind. Then, tragedy struck. A receptionist interrupted class to bring Virginia an urgent message from Rabbit. She needed to call home immediately. Rabbit shared the news that Rhonda had been involved in a horrible automobile accident. She had been airlifted to a hospital in Colorado Springs and they needed to leave immediately. Rabbit and Virginia met at the Tulsa airport to catch the next flight. Treacherous weather in Colorado threatened take off, but eventually the pilot received the all clear. They flew in the blizzard and landing was precarious. Rabbit knew all to well the dangers of zero visibility and a potentially slick runway. The pilot in him made remaining in his seat the hardest thing to do. He would have felt much more comfortable in the cockpit.

The plane landed safely just as the Colorado Springs airport closed all runways. It was the final flight allowed to land in the storm. The Hares hurried up the jet bridge to find Rhonda's husband waiting, accompanied by a friend who drove a four-wheel drive truck.

Rhonda's injuries were critical and extensive. No one knew if she would be alive when they reached the hospital. Few words were spoken across the fifteen-mile distance that seemed impossible to travel. The driving snow was no match for the passengers' pounding hearts. The truck's big tires passed stranded motorists who didn't arrive at their destinations soon enough to beat the storm. Relief washed over the truck's occupants when they gained sight of the hospital, then faded as the four-wheel-drive made several attempts to climb the incline of the drive. The heavy-duty tires only spun out and slid back down. The trio, hoping they would find Rhonda alive, thanked their chauffeur as they jumped from the cab and crawled up the icy, snow covered hill to the hospital doors .

Rabbit and Virginia couldn't recognize their daughter. The car's steering wheel had protected most of the major organs in her torso. Everything else was crushed and swollen. Her head was three times its normal size. Bones were broken in hundreds of places. Only time would reveal the full extent of her injuries.

Rhonda amazed the doctors with her Hare fighting spirit. She clung to the very edge of life and gradually stabilized. As soon as the swelling subsided, the work of putting her back together began. Surgeries repaired her bones; physical therapy returned strength and eventually mobility. Recovery from her head trauma would only happen with the notable Hare determination, and it required help from the entire family.

Rhonda had to learn to talk, eat, read, and write again. It took more strength and resolve than she possessed at times. It required the willpower of Rabbit to not allow her to give up, the fortitude of Virginia to encourage her to keep working, and the aptitude of her sisters and brother to challenge her to do more.

Virginia's long months by Rhonda's hospital bedside both flew by and dragged on. Hours of sitting, waiting, and comforting were followed by flurries of activity around surgeries and therapy. The possibility of repeating a semester of school was just a fact Virginia had to deal with. However, her professors amazed her with an outpouring of support for their top student.

They suspended the work from her classes and allowed her to complete the courses whenever she could.

Rhonda walked a long, slow road toward healing, and after some time, Virginia continued her fast track toward teaching.

When it came time to practice student teaching, the elementary level attracted Virginia to the cute little minds so eager to learn. It didn't take long for her to decide the secondary level would be a better fit. The 1980's brought a shortage of teachers for students with special needs. Recruiters set their sights on Virginia, who decided the challenge would be worth the reward. She obtained certifications in mental retardation, learning disabilities, and language arts K-12. Graduation day finally arrived.

Virginia's petite frame stood straight and tall draped in her long, black graduation gown. The warm May evening in 1980 hosted family and friends who came to celebrate the college degree thirty years in the making. This was a day truly worth celebrating. Virginia felt the presence of her children, who consistently encouraged her pursuit, but couldn't be there in person. After graduating from the same university five years before, Allan was on assignment with the Tulsa World newspaper. Rhonda was still recovering from her car accident. Bunni and Valerie brought enough cheers and love for them all.

The graduates in Virginia's row stood and filed toward the steps leading to the stage. Movement across the field caught Virginia's attention. It was Allan walking toward the back of the stage with camera in hand. Delighted by the surprise, a smile overtook Virginia's face as she accepted her diploma from Dr. Collier with Allan in position to capture the moment. To the delight of the audience, the commencement speaker, Congressman Mike Synar, chided Allan for his back door entry.

When the celebration ended, the ever-present picture frame welcomed Virginia's graduation photograph. Only it wasn't Ruth who placed the new photo in the legendary frame. She had died two months earlier. From an early age, Virginia shared Ruth's desire to pursue opportunities, high standards, and meaningful experiences. Ruth died knowing Virginia would fulfill her dream, and Virginia graduated with Ruth's ever-present spirit as a constant companion. The last of two generations to receive her degree, Virginia persevered to the end, which was really a new beginning.

Dami Phi Reunions

By the time the children were grown, Ira had amassed the fortune he always promised Mary Lou. Investing in construction and real estate, Ira had built an impressive business and made quite a name for himself in certain circles. He began building stunning houses for Mary Lou – perfect settings for weeklong Dami Phi Datum reunions.

The first extended reunion took place in 1981 at the Fulton Family lodge in Pinetop, Arizona. Stately pine trees stood guard over the ladies as they enjoyed long walks with squirrels darting across the path. Cool breezes magnified the lovely scent of the pines. The rustic luxury relaxed their bodies while being among dear friends sparked memories and endless conversations.

The week ended much too soon and inspired Martha to produce volume two of the Dami Phi News as a tribute. The Dami Phi News second volume was published August 31, 1981. The staff at the publication hadn't changed in the thirty-two years between printings. The masthead listed Martha Martin as Editor, Business Manager, Reporter, and Publisher. The Second Edition of a "World Famous Paper" opened with a letter from the editor, who else but Martha Martin.

> The original intent when I sent out requests for everyone to write their thoughts on the reunion was that I would publish only those thoughts; but the letters that came with those thoughts are worth sharing, so I have decided to put it all in the NEWS in the order in which I received them.

VIRGINIA ON ABUNDANT LIFE

> Martha, Here's the OPS (Okie Press System) release on the DPD Reunion. Please feel free to add, delete, or change at will. Looking forward to the Second Edition!
>
> "The whispering pines of northern Arizona lulled and blended with giggles, shrieks, and non-stop vocalizing as Dami Phi Datum gathered in Pinetop for their

first grandiose reunion in thirty-one years.

Situated midst this rustic setting, the cottage of Mary Lou and Ira Fulton provided all the finer comforts of home as the reminiscing, scrapbook 'n photo sharing, picture-snapping, gourmet cooking, and partying continued on an almost 24-hour basis throughout the five-day reunion.

Gathering from the far flung corners of Oklahoma, Texas, Arizona, and California, the six former high school buddies found no shortage of conversation topics ... the main challenge being to "tune in" to several exchanges at one time so as not to miss any choice morsels or jolting reminders from depths of mind ... as one story triggered still another.

While the ensuing years have added character (and beauty) to their faces, maturity to their judgment, and a softening thoughtfulness to their thinking, their voices have retained their uniqueness of quality and the ability to endure.

Through the bond of enduring friendship and continuing communication, these members of Dami Phi Datum have "invested" in life. Through this investment has manifested richness of life – a life that is beautiful, a life that is truly abundant. – Virginia"

MARY LOU AND CUTLERY DELIGHTS

Editors Note: Mary Lou was so busy fixing and furnishing her new mountain home that she didn't have time to write her thoughts; so she called them in like a good cub reporter would. Therefore, the following report are her thoughts as written and commented on by me ... who else but ... Martha Martin.

"Naturally having been on a diet for the last decade I was most impressed with our culinary delights. Snookie and Ginger masterminded the tastiest of banana cakes. There was banana cake #1, and banana cake #2; both were taste heaven, but perhaps #1 was somewhat better than #2, as #2 didn't quite finish baking."

EDITORS NOTE: Then of course,

there were peanut butter sandwiches!

"A lot of time and preparation were spent by the Nacho Queen, Barbara, as she sorted chips, grated cheese, sliced jalapenos, and spread the refried beans for the greatest Mexican taste treat north of El Paso."

EDITORS NOTE: Then of course, there were peanut butter sandwiches!

"Snookie's greatest delight came with a wonderful palate treat – the stir-fries. Smelled great cooking, tasted great going down, remembered great in our after thoughts."

NOTE: Then of course, there were peanut butter sandwiches!

"The piece de resistance came from Ira, with a gourmet trip out for Prime Rib and Cordon Bleu. This mouth-watering experience included a complete salad bar, wine, and a meat treat to equal the best anywhere."

E.N.: And then of course, there were peanut butter sandwiches!

"The culinary delights were all so memorable, as were the two mile evening hikes, Virginia and Snookie with their morning coffee on the porch, Shirley, poor dear, feeling bad the first day, the squirrels, the birds, the chipmunks, and of course, dear Ira and his sweet bouquets of flowers. But the most unbelievable part of all, is that after thirty-one years no one had really changed. – Mary Lou"

MARTHA HAS A BIRTHDAY PARTY

"August 2, 1981 – Martha Martin, referred to in a previous Dami Phi paper as Moron Martin, was awaking in a mountain cabin in Pinetop, Arizona belonging to Mary Lou and husband Ira. The day dawned with anticipation and excitement, for it was the second day of the GREAT reunion.

Martha hurried to the kitchen to find Barbara working diligently with a can of frozen O.J. Snookie and Virginia were up to their elbows in great banana cake making. Martha lent a hand at bacon and egg cooking, and once the great cake was in the oven the breakfast was eaten.

The day passed with great merriment and companionship. A trip to the flea market was great fun, but only because we were together. Barbara did a wonderful job of providing Nachos for lunch, and the evening found us too full for a complete dinner, so everyone prepared whatever sounded good to them for their dinner snack.

Martha was absorbed in T.V. when suddenly came the sounds of five voices singing Happy Birthday, and five friends carrying the banana cake with candles in the shape of forty-nine ... and as if that wasn't the greatest surprise of a lifetime, presents were also in evidence. Lots of picture taking followed while Martha blew out the candles. In fact, so much picture taking took place that the candles had to be relit three or four times, to the point that the candle wax was melted all over the cake. It was therefore, put in the freezer to harden while Martha opened her gifts ... a box of notepaper, a box of candy turtles, a stoneware vase, and a puzzle that to this date has never been back to its original form.

What a wonderful birthday party
... friends from thirty-one years ago
to say they cared with cake and gifts.
THANK YOU GUYS --- I'LL NEVER
FORGET IT!!!!!! – Martha"

SHIRLEY DIDN'T EXPECT TO ATTEND

"Dear Martha,

Thought maybe I'd better try and get something off to you now because when you put it out of sight it goes out of mind, and October would be here before I knew it. Is someone making a copy for all of us on the first paper? Sure hope so! Wasn't that funny? Wish I'd kept more things like that, but we've moved so much. Hope this item isn't too long. Really appreciate your effort on this paper. Tell Ann hello for me, and I'd love to be doing a puzzle now. Any more "Uno" lately?

I hadn't let the excitement build for the reunion because I knew there was no way we could afford for me to go. So when Mary Lou called to see if I was coming because "everyone else would be there" and she and Ira offered to pay my way, I was happy, to say the least. The excitement still didn't reach me until Saturday morning when I saw all of you together and realized, 'Hey, I'm in Phoenix with that ole gang of mine.' Happy Day! So many things from my past are lost due to my mom losing all our old photographs. Also, where I lived on Seventeenth and Jefferson being torn down, even the sidewalk with my name put there at age five had been redone. Nothing from the past lingered except --- friendships with some pretty special gals. I'm so thankful I didn't miss it!! The special banana cake for Martha's birthday! The lovely flowers to welcome us! The sharing deeper of one another's lives than in letters, what a joy!! The one thing which brings laughter and tears is when Snookie, Virginia, Barb, and I were returning and on the outskirts of Mesa realized we'd all been to Camp Wamatochick in Prescott as Camp Fire Girls and burst out in "Ki Yi Ki Like Us, Nobody Like Us, We Are The Girls From

Camp Wamatochick." Where else could you bring good ole memories back like that?

The Lord has been good to all of us through the years and I'm thankful to have made such wonderful enduring friends such as all of you!!!! Course there is ONE who will hit fifty first, but she holds her age well – as well as the rest of us!!!! – Shirley"

BARBARA GIVES US THE A. B. C.'S OF IT

"Martha,

Are you nuts? In 1949, you asked for help on "the paper" and didn't get none. So what do you expect thirty-two years later? You know we haven't changed – HOWEVER, I will try – HOWEVER, you mentioned October 1, but failed to mention a year, twice, so I am using that to my advantage. Also you failed to dot your eyes and cross t's in the word writings so – that is ten points off. HOWEVER, it is a great idea so .., I'll try. Wait till you see the pictures of your party – SUPER!!

A – Arizona, our roots

B – Banana cakes, indescribably delicious

C – Cooks who cooked calories, yum!

D – Dami Phi Newspaper, a gut buster

E – Everything that goes up, does not necessarily come down – anymore.

F – Fellowship unknown
by any other group

G – Good, good photos and a fun hamburger puzzle, with sesame seeds

H – Hospitality unmatched
from LuLu and Ira

I – Incessant yakking

J – Jokes and laughter and
screeching and screaming

K – Kept the Round Robin orbiting for thirty-one years

L – Loved those annuals

M – Mouse in the house

N – Near the beautiful birds,
animals, trees, and sky

O – Oh! That wonderful mountain home was restful

P – Peanut Butter – we
thank you Laura Scudder
Q – Quite a birthday party – now
how old did you say Martha??
R – Reminiscing of good
old P.U.H.S. days
S – School cheers and
songs Rah! Rah! Rah!
T – Toast to the memories
U – Uno = Yuck-o!
V – Viva la Dami Phi Datums
W – Walking was invigorating
X – X-ray our hearts and
see love for one another
Y – Year was 1981
Z – Zippety Doo Da, zippety ay,
my, oh my, what a joyous five days
Wonderful feelings, wonderful walks
Let's get together for some
more talks. – Barbara"

SNOOKIE REMINISCES

"Hi Martha, Am I last? I gave
this a great deal of thought; you
see – Now to set it on paper.
All this brought me so much pleasure,
and the memories continue to do so:
Early mornings on the porch with Mary
Lou's animals, Virginia, and coffee.
Walks both before and after dark.
Ira's determination that we enjoy
and his solicitude in making sure.
Smiles come when I think of:
Shopping for groceries
Martha's surprise birthday party
Convening in bedrooms, bathrooms,
kitchen, wherever, with the gab never
letting up (and the concern over miss-
ing something in the next room!)
Barb doing 'On Coy-
otes' all the way through!
Martha, Ann, and I al-
ways bringing up the rear.

In pondering, I cannot believe that as diverse as our life paths have been, even though we have communicated these many years, that we did not run out of things to talk about even after five days. Martha, I told you about discovering that all of us in the car had gone to Camp Wamatochick as we were approaching Phoenix coming home, didn't I?

I found our time together a cleansing of the soul in a way, even without Kitty-cat Court and with the feeling, once it was over, that you all are probably my very best friends in the world.

I feel undying gratitude to Mary Lou and Ira for making this possible. Just where did the five days go?

Also, the bonus I wish to mention, getting better acquainted with Ann, what a dear person! I do hope she didn't leave thinking us completely nuts! We did so enjoy her presence.

There are few times in a person's life that you recognize as a highlight while it is happening, this time together was one of those. Don't you think everyone was aware of how special it was?

A mystery to me is that fact that we really did not touch on personal lives, other than children; husbands, marriages, philosophies came up very seldom. Gives us something to discuss next reunion!!! – Snookie"

Martha's guest at the reunion, Ann, contributed a small part to the Dami Phi News as well.

A POEM FROM ANN

"High school reunions seem to
be a part of everyone's fate;
Sometimes they are funny, sometimes
they are sad, but always they are great.
So when time comes for mine,
and I'm feeling sublime,
I hope it's as fine as the
Dami Phi kind. – Ann"

It was four years before the next Dami Phi retreat. In 1985, they all met at Mary Lou's home in Mesa, Arizona. The reunions were such a hit;

the girls decided they must become an annual affair. The friends used the Round Robin letters to plan months in advance. Mary Lou coordinated wonderful activities and everyone pitched in with grocery shopping, celebration ideas, and a special hostess gift for Mary Lou. All of the ladies loved the experiences they shared and looked for creative ways to contribute to the group's enjoyment and express gratitude to Mary Lou.

The reunions allowed Mary Lou to return to her giggling, schoolgirl days, a welcome break from her growing position in society. While Mary Lou let her hair down, the other girls lived it up. They each relaxed in private bedrooms and enjoyed the service of housekeepers, cooks, and drivers. Mary Lou's cousin, Bill, often drove and escorted the ladies on excursions. He enjoyed the silliness and laughter as much as the girls and proved to be a knowledgeable tour guide.

Reunions were hosted in new locations as Ira and Mary Lou added to the Fulton real estate portfolio. Each new home was bigger and grander than the one before. The couple's generosity became legendary among the Dami Phi friends who bathed in luxury in mansions in Mesa, Pinetop, Prescott, and Ahwatukee, Arizona, Chatsworth and Coronado Island, California, and Provo, Utah.

The ocean breezes and soft, sandy beaches of Coronado quickly became everyone's favorite and saw the group return for seven reunions. Pacific views from the front veranda drew them outside for morning coffee. Snookie and Virginia eagerly filled all of the unscheduled minutes with walks on the beach where they laughed and talked above the sounds of the waves.

The girls assigned each reunion a theme from "Hats on Parade" to "Leis, Luaus, and Mumus." The number of days scheduled for the reunion directly correlated with the height of the piles of luggage. Each member of Dami Phi Datum packed for every contingency and gave the appointed valet a nice workout. Virginia brought extra boxes to the 1997 reunion to teach her friends how to create beautiful scrapbook pages. They spent hours reliving memories from the photos they brought, creating themes for pages, and journaling thoughts and stories from the occasions. Virginia soon became known as the Scrapbooking Queen who had an album for all of life's events.

Twenty-one years of reunions provided the friends with countless stories and a treasure of wonderful memories before age and health prompted them to make the 2012 Coronado reunion the last. Now, Virginia's scrapbooks keep the historical account of the Dami Phi adventures. Every page brings a flood of memories and knowing smiles to the faces of these devoted friends.

Dami Phi Legacy

The legacy inspired by Virginia's life is recorded in a multitude of scrapbooks. The thick bindings bulge with inserted newspaper clippings and notes wedged between the decorated pages. They do not sit on a shelf gathering dust. They keep Virginia company on snowy days by the fire and late nights when sleep won't come. They remind her of a blessed life with extraordinary friends and a loyal family.

Another part of her legacy is recorded in high school yearbooks. Virginia's early dreams and memories always centered on teaching. She loved all of her teachers. They were kind and inspiring. Virginia remembers special weekends with her second grade teacher, Guida Smith. Miss Smith lived with her parents in Mesa, only two doors down from the then only Mormon Temple in Arizona. What a treat it was for her to spend the weekend exploring new surroundings and bathing in the full attention of Miss Smith and her family. Virginia maintained contact with many of her teachers through correspondence even after leaving Phoenix.

Education went through many changes before Virginia became Ms. Hare to everyone in Jay, Oklahoma who had not yet graduated high school. Virginia believed an effective teacher knew her students beyond their test scores and cared about all aspects of their life. She knew she could teach a blind man to play accordion and she believed she could teach special needs students to become valued members of the community. Virginia saw each student's capabilities, not limitations.

Learning to work and hold a job was an important aspect of Virginia's teaching philosophy. She had done her intern teaching with the work-study program and was then hired to teach the program. By the time the students started a part-time job the second semester, they knew how to dress, relate with other people, arrive on time, punch a time clock, and accept responsibilities. Virginia often encountered former students about town who proudly announced, "Ms. Hare, I have a job! I'm working!"

By the time the specially selected juniors and seniors reached Ms. Hare's high school classroom, they had learned a strong sense of mistrust and built high walls of defenses to protect themselves from negative comments and failure. Virginia taught algebra, English, reading, and science as well as patriotism, responsibility, time management, and interpersonal skills. She also invested great effort in building trust among classmates. Larry Renegar, director of Rocmnd Youth Services, visited Virginia's class weekly. He sat on the floor with the students and led games that required peer interaction and built trust. This important life-skill eventually allowed them to begin trusting classmates and more easily transition into trusting employers and co-workers.

Virginia took her students to a ropes course, led them on trust walks, and exposed them to all available opportunities, much like her mother did for her. They prepared for the Special Olympics with training and fundraisers. Famed Oklahoma University football coach Barry Switzer accompanied the Special Olympics team every four years to places like the University of Notre Dame, New York City, and Baton Rouge for participation in national events. He motivated the athletes and encouraged them to do their best. One of Virginia's students, Jeff, was selected as Special Olympian of the Year for Oklahoma and had the opportunity of a lifetime. He carried the Olympic torch through the streets of Tulsa, Oklahoma on its way to Los Angeles, the summer of 1984.

After discovering most of her students had never gone to a prom or any other dance, Virginia set out to change that. She made sure her students could intellectually purchase prom tickets, knew dance etiquette, and learned proper attire. She leveraged all of her resources to find dresses and suits and even volunteered to chaperone the dance. Although Rabbit and Virginia began their relationship moving across the dance floor to the music of the 1950s, Rabbit thought his dancing shoes might not make the transition to 1980s music. Rabbit stayed home this time while Virginia worked overtime. Known for his fabulous skill and enjoyment of dancing, fellow teacher, Stan Starts became Virginia's faithful prom date. She kept a watchful eye on her children. Experiencing all life had to offer was important for them – just as it had been for Virginia.

All of the activities, training, and confidence Virginia guided her students through culminated in one graduation activity. Spelunking. The maze of caves in southwest Missouri expanded and contracted with little warning. Virginia joined her students on hands and knees -- crawling through tight spaces, climbing steep, rocky inclines, and twisting bodies to navigate through mud and bat droppings. Tired, dirty students faced a two-story chimney pipe, daring them to scale it midway. The cave's exit was small, requiring laying on one's back and inching out through the narrow horizontal opening.

Virginia noted one student, Jason, thought he had reached his physical and emotional limit before encountering the vertical pipe. The defeated young man sat below the pipe and gave into the tears pushing behind his eyes. As Jason sat and cried, Virginia worked her way past him and began to shimmy up the pipe yelling over her shoulder, "Jason, look at this old lady. If I can do this, so can you!"

Jason looked through his tears to see hints of sunlight streaming around Virginia's silver hair, and he knew he had to try. Using arms, legs, knees, and back, Jason inched his way up the pipe. He finished as a changed young man. Restrictions and limitations lifted, and Jason believed in himself as Virginia believed in him all along.

After dedicating herself to improving the lives of her students for sixteen years, Virginia finally retired. Her Dami Phi friends were ready to celebrate her career at the next reunion and planned a grand surprise party. After a short time out of the classroom, Virginia began to receive requests from her daughter Valerie who taught biology and chemistry at the high school in Grove, Oklahoma. Valerie needed a substitute teacher who could continue instruction in her absence. Soon, Valerie's coworkers requested Virginia to substitute for them as well. Virginia filled-in over weeks for maternity leave as well as random single days. A decade later, she finally ended her teaching career with satisfaction and contentment, knowing her students were encouraged and well equipped for the future.

Virginia retired from education, but she continued to teach and learn, especially with Rabbit. After having built together their novel, earth-bermed, efficient home on Grand Lake, the duo decided to build an airplane in the three-car garage.

They took several years to decide on a two-place GlaStar kit by Stoddard Hamilton. It employed the best all-round features that they wanted – a steel framed cage cockpit, metal wings, fiberglass body, and a large cargo area for camping gear.

Virginia assisted Rabbit in every endeavor from wiring to wing construction, but she refused to buck rivets. The process of setting the pins in place involved compressing the head against a bucking bar on the shank side. When the shank has nowhere to go, it expands outward to form another head. This seemed like work for Rabbit and another helper to do while she chronicled the building progress in a scrapbook.

During the GlaStar construction project, Rabbit fell from a deer tree stand. His injuries left Virginia flying solo for a while. The fall pulverized both of his wrists, broke his nose, ribs, and elbow. Virginia continued working inside the aircraft shell, crawling inside the fuse-lodge to do Rabbit's bidding on wiring, and following all of his detailed instructions.

Rabbit's accident slowed the building process, but the Hares still managed to complete the project in less than three years. On July 2, 1999, Rabbit soloed the homebuilt aircraft with the call sign of N866RH. The tail number had significant meaning to Rabbit. The F-80 he flew in Korea was 866 and RH, of course was for Rabbit Hare. A few days later, the two flew the GlaStar to Oshkosh for the Experimental Aircraft Association Air Adventure. It is one of the largest air shows in the world and always the Hares' favorite.

The GlaStar transported Rabbit and Virginia to many adventures that always involved reconnecting with old friends. The Hares lives crossed the paths of many others with whom Virginia faithfully corresponded. Retirement years were booked mostly with reunions and family gatherings. Rabbit took off for his final flight west in 2010, as he and Virginia anticipated their fifty-ninth wedding anniversary. Virginia waved, "So long for now," and marches ever onward experiencing new adventures, carrying his memory with her every step of the way.

The flight paths taken by the Dami Phi's were diverse and varied but their destinations shared the results of the common values that bound the friends together. With the exception of Martha, who never married, each Dami Phi had only one husband with long-time marriages. Snookie and Gene, Barbara and Gene, Shirley and Bob, and Mary Lou and Ira all have celebrated 60th wedding anniversaries. That's monumental in anybody's book!

The girls have laughed and shared along the way, blessing others with their mindfulness toward life. In varied ways, they continue to give, volunteer, inspire, and teach. They believe in strong families, lead by example, strength of purpose, and a determination to see things through while giving their families a true sense of belonging and love never-ending.

The round Robin letters continue to circulate among these special friends because tradition is important. However, the letters have slowed considerably as the convenience of e-mail has drawn them into its web of expediency. They catch-up often, now that cell phones have come into play.

For sixty-seven years the Dami Phi's have encouraged and supported one another, laughing along the way, finding the best in one another and life itself. Their deep friendship is like a rainbow. When the perfect amounts of happiness and tears mix, the result is a colorful bridge between hearts. Each one, her own unique color, but when knit closely together they blend in perfect complement to form new, beautiful colors.

The Dami Phi Datum girls no longer have the agility to pile into that 1939 Chevy coupe with the bench seat. They still enjoy riding in one of

Mary Lou's luxury cars with a chauffeur driving them about on new adventures while they giggle, chatter, and cherish always the long time friendship they've shared.

-- THE END --

Afterword – Where Are They Now?

Virginia's brother Mickey, a kind soul, lover of life, and true gentleman, enjoyed a thirty-five year career as a pilot for American Airlines. His daughters Katy and Maggie soared in his jet stream, also becoming pilots for major airlines as well as marrying pilots. Mickey lost his wife Betsy in 1995. Five years later he retired to Carefree, Arizona where he continued to fly his shiny Cessna 1-40 and enjoy his grandchildren; Betsy, Will, and Emerson. After a valiant battle with cancer spanning a period of sixteen years, Virginia's brother Mickey 'flew west' on February 15, 2015, making his transition. His ashes were spread on his beloved Mingus Mountain where he once hunted deer as a teenager.

In 2009, Virginia's sister, Patricia retired from teaching after thirty-two years in a Mesa, Arizona classroom. Patricia's teaching career included teaching remedial reading to high school kids and being chair of the reading department at Red Mountain High School. She accomplished amazing feats and received a number of awards. Included among her accomplishments and awards are Point of Light award, received from president George Bush; Arizona Citizen of the year awarded by Arizona's major TV/media corporations; Top Five Most Innovative Teachers in the United States, awarded by the National Education Association; Power of One award presented by Senator John McCain; Most Outstanding High School Service Club in the nation, awarded by the National Education Channel; and, Volunteer of the Year awarded by Reading is Fundamental (RIF), the nation's largest literacy organization.

Patricia had the distinction of leading the largest Club RIF in the nation, with 1800 card-carrying members from a high school student body of 2000. Her program, Club RIF, has become the model for service learning programs for high schools throughout the nation. Patricia is continuing her literacy Club activities with high school alumni.

Patricia continues to twirl her baton at alumni events at a slightly slower pace than when she was Arizona State Champion. Patricia lives with her husband Skip in Gilbert, Arizona where they celebrated their 50th wedding anniversary in 2014. She and Skip enjoy traveling the back roads of Arizona and out of the way places. They have two children, Andrea and Chris and five grandchildren, Brennan, Regan, Casey, Tyler, and Thomas.

Shirley achieved her dream of having a large family gather around the dinner table. She and Bob have six children, Debbie, Craig, Brenda, Deanna, and the twins Brad and Brent. For a time, Shirley enjoyed a great sense of making a difference in individual lives by teaching babies and small children to swim. After living as a pastor's family in Arizona, Washington, Texas, California, and South Africa, they established roots in Oracle, Arizona. Shirley had the opportunity to work several years at the University of Arizona's Biosphere project while Bob assumed the senior minister position at a newly formed church. In 2007, Bob semi-retired but continues to teach a Wednesday night Bible class.

They enjoy thirteen grandchildren and seventeen great grandchildren.

Barbara married Gene Smith in 1952, and then graduated from ASU two years later with her degree in Elementary Education. They moved from Phoenix to El Paso in 1957, where they lived for fifty-three years and raised their two children, Mark and Linda. Barbara retired in 1987 from the El Paso Independent School District after twenty-eight years as a first grade teacher and reading specialist. Gene worked as a U.S. probation officer until his retirement in 1992. In 2010, they moved to Fort Worth, Texas to be closer to Linda and her husband Bill. Barbara and Gene have four grandchildren and one great-grandchild. Gene made his transition to Gloryland March 25, 2015.

Mary Lou and Ira moved from California back to Arizona in 1974, and began developing the Fulton Homes Corporation. Their company ultimately grew into one of the largest home building businesses in Arizona. Mary Lou and Ira graciously provided the location for the Dami Phi reunions for over thirty years. Along the way, they have become one of Arizona's largest education philanthropists. Arizona State University and Brigham Young University are the primary recipients of the Fulton's investment in education. Mary Lou and Ira had three children, Lori, Greg, and Doug. They lost Greg to ALS in 2011. They enjoy sixteen grandchildren and several great grandchildren.

Martha enjoyed her retirement from the Frazee Paint Company traveling the United States and Mexico. Eventually she bought a home in Scottsdale, Arizona. She settled there with her two wire-haired Dachshunds, Sara and Rosie, plus one talking bird to keep her company. She hosted several impromptu Dami Phi reunions when her Dami Phi friends showed up in the Valley of the Sun. Martha made her transition to Gloryland from there in 2006. Her presence and her sense of humor were sorely missed whenever the Dami Phi's gathered.

After Snookie went back to Lamson's Business College for refresher courses and shorthand classes, she started her career in the early 1980s. Her interest in politics led her to the Arizona House of Representative. She was assigned administrative duties for a newly elected representative, Carl Kunsek, a pharmacy owner from Mesa. Snookie and Carl got along well and enjoyed learning the intricacies of the system together. Carl's political career grew from junior representative to committee member to Senator chairing the Health Committee and finally, Senate president. Snookie stayed by his side throughout the journey experiencing her own whirlwind of excitement. A secretary to share some of Snookie's responsibilities came with the advancement to a big office that was the central hub for activity. Snookie juggled requests from constituents and lobbyists pouring through the front door as well as activity through the back door's steady stream of aides, staff, and guards along with Senators popping in frequently.

The intensity and excitement of Snookie's job increased exponentially when Arizona's first impeachment trial hit the doorstep of Senator Kunsek's office. The state attorney general charged Morman Governor Karl Mecham with campaign finance violations and obstruction of justice. Supreme Court Chief Justice was Presiding Officer. Attorneys were everywhere; prosecuting attorney, defense attorney, and their staffs. Snookie remembers the near constant ringing of the phone, the excitement from early morning to late evening, and total exhaustion at the end of each day.

Governor Mecham was impeached, indicted, and subjected to a recall campaign. Following the negative exposure from the impeachment trial, Senator Kunsek did not win his re-election bid. Snookie felt this was Mesa's big loss as most in the Senate found Carl to be most fair, honest, and open-minded in his dealings. Snookie left politics too and began working in a doctor's office where she sustained a stroke and was forced to retire.

In 1999, she and Gene sold their Phoenix home and moved to Tucson to be closer to both their children, Jennie and Kelly, and two grandsons, Andrew and Daniel.

Rabbit made his final flight in January 7, 2010, after a distinguished career in the Air Force. He enjoyed his retirement building the

GlaStar and then flying it wherever the skies beckoned. He taught each of his children and two grandchildren to fly, establishing a strong Hare aviation heritage. He enjoyed spending time with his grandchildren jug fishing, riding four-wheelers, and enjoying life.

The turmoil of the stormy skies on the day of Rabbit's funeral matched the blustering emotions in Virginia's heart as she said goodbye to her life's co-pilot. Virginia felt comforted by the grand send-off for her World War II, Korea, and Vietnam veteran. The bugler sounding Taps seemed to bring sadness from God himself as the low clouds met with the rising fog. Pilots from Rabbit's Quiet Birdmen (QB) Joplin, Missouri hanger went to great lengths to honor and respect Rabbit in his passing with a fly-by in spite of the weather conditions. The racing aircraft engines, including Rabbit's own GlaStar, welcomed Rabbit home.

Rabbit began teaching Virginia how to be alone while she was still a bride. He consciously equipped her for independence while he flew combat and covert missions through the years.

He discussed plans and actions she should take in his absence. Virginia practiced dependence on her faith with each passing day, never expecting a life-long marriage, but grateful for the blessings of every moment.

The independence Rabbit encouraged strengthens Virginia as she continues to live in her home on the shores of Grand Lake O' the Cherokees. The grass strip beckons the occasional plane for a fly-by. Two daughters, Rhonda and Valerie, live within twenty-five miles of their mother. Son Allan lives in Tulsa and frequently arrives at the lake to mow and enjoy the pleasures of his childhood lake home. Oldest daughter, Bunni, lives in Australia ---just a long airplane ride away. Six grandchildren, Ashley, Aaron, Emily, Andrew, Sarah, and Gregorye, plus the greats, Grayden and Maisie, enjoy the adventurous fun that always accompanies grandmother Virginia.

Virginia utilizes all her flying privileges, every one, forever on the go to Air Force and school reunions, American Legion Auxiliary conventions, and visiting vintage friends. Virginia's life shares the widespread roots of the cactus flower easily bringing beauty to the desert and adding wonder to the mountains. Like the cactus, she is a survivor, hardy and resilient having lived life fully. Her constant good expectations gave her a life overflowing with remarkable, enduring friendships. She embraces generous portions of family, love, and the harmony God provides.

Acknowledgements

A great big thank you to Ashley, my dental hygienist, who told this writer, "Hey, my grandmother has a lot of stories to tell," and Virginia who entrusted me to write some of them. Hats off to Virginia's amazing recollection of names and details.

Much appreciation to the finest at their craft, Mary Thornton and Sharon Derwin Watson, who read manuscripts with thoughtful attention to detail. This book is better because of your editing.

To the members of Dami Phi Datum who willingly became vulnerable, shared memories, corrected details, and allowed me to attend parties; thank you Shirley, Barbara, Mary Lou, and Snookie.

Thanks to Patricia for the fantastic tacos and hysterical stories that allowed me a broader view of the Howell family.

I'll never forget Snookie driving Virginia and I around Phoenix where all of the familiar streets have changed. U-turns were never so fun.

Scott Horton, thank you for allowing me to read chapters to you. Your patience and encouragement are invaluable, and your designs wow me every time. You are my perfect partner.

Preslie, my sidekick and cheerleader, your prayers keep me going. The way you delight in all of our meetings with Virginia gives me joy.

Virginia, your 'short story' could never fit that description. This full-length work has been worth all of the hours to gain your friendship. I've never met anyone who values friends as much as you. My life is richer because you are in it.

Cheerio,

Sarah Horton

CPSIA information can be obtained
at www.ICGtesting.com
Printed in the USA
FFOW05n0910221015

9 780988 585089